Non-verbal Reasoning

TESTBOOK **3**

Standard & Multiple-choice 30 Minute Tests

Dr Stephen C Curran
with Andrea Richardson
Edited by Autumn McMahon

This book belongs to

Accelerated Education Publications Ltd

Guidance notes for parents

These practice papers can be completed as standard or multiple-choice tests.

Multiple-choice Tests

Answers are entered onto the answer sheets at the back of the book. The actual test would be marked by a computer but, for the purposes of these practice tests, you will need to mark it yourself. It is important for your child to treat it like the real thing and record an answer in the appropriate box by drawing a clear line through their chosen box with a pencil. Mistakes should be carefully rubbed out and not crossed out since in the actual test this would not be correctly recorded by the computer.

Standard Tests

Ask your child to circle the answers as instructed in each section. Mistakes should be crossed through with a single line and the correct answer written clearly.

Marking and Feedback

The answers are provided at the back of this book. Only these answers are allowed. One mark should be given for each correct answer. Do not deduct marks for wrong answers. Do not allow half marks or 'the benefit of the doubt', as this might mask a child's need for extra help in the topic and does not replicate the real exam conditions. Always try to be positive and encouraging. Talk through any mistakes with your child and work out together how to arrive at the right answer.

Timing

This testbook contains 8 practice papers. Each paper should take about 30 minutes, however it is more important that a child completes the paper accurately and does not rush their answers. Children will speed up naturally with practice.

Non-verbal Reasoning Test 1

Section A

To the left of each of the lines below there are five squares arranged in order. One of these squares has been left empty. Find which one of the five squares on the right should take the place of the empty square.

Example

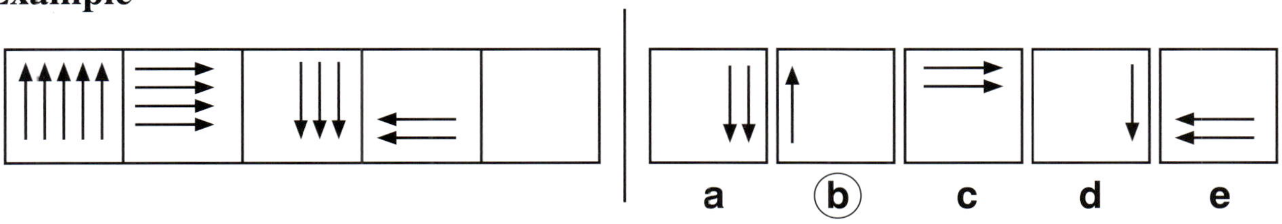

a (b) c d e

Now do the questions below. Circle the correct answer.

1)

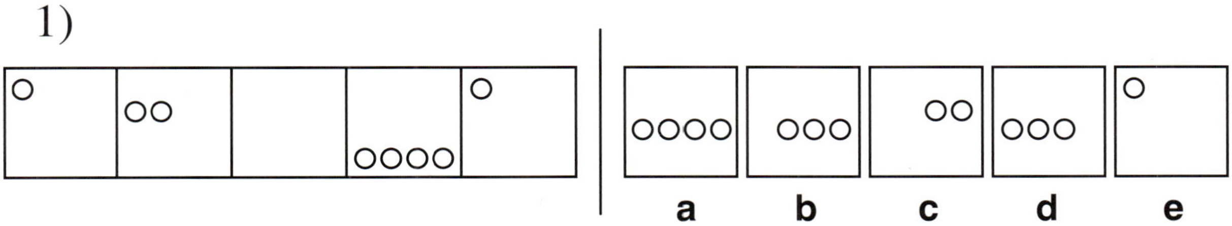

a b c d e

2)

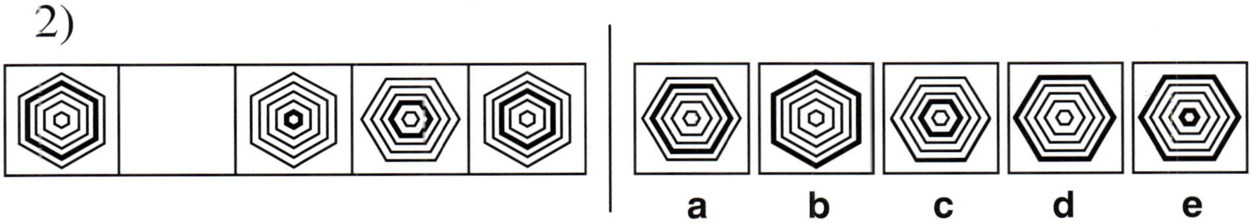

a b c d e

3)

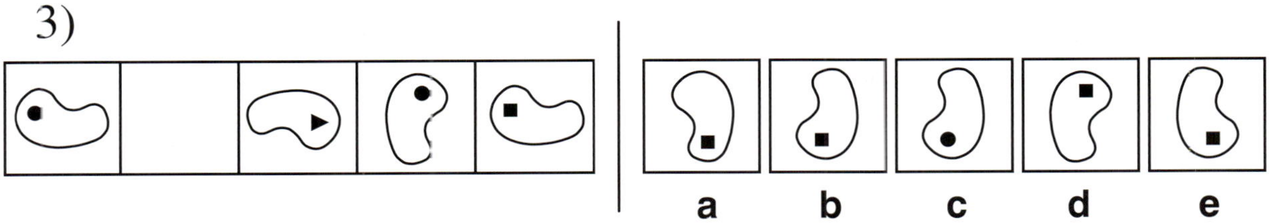

a b c d e

4)

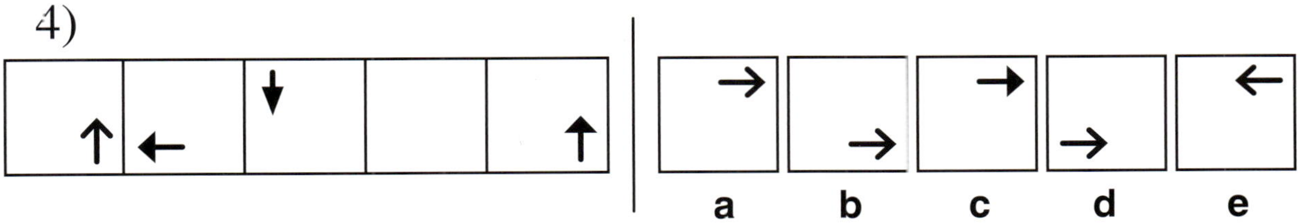

a b c d e

5)

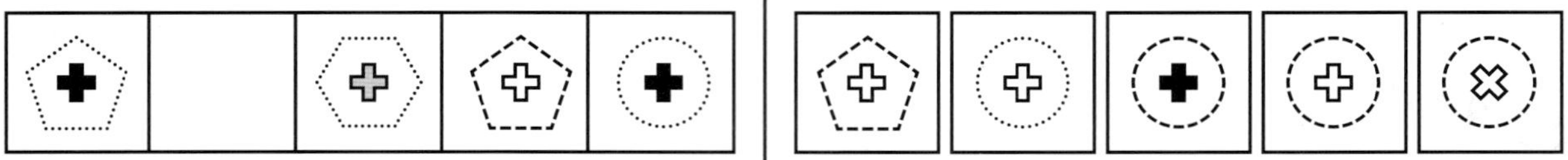

a b c d e

6)

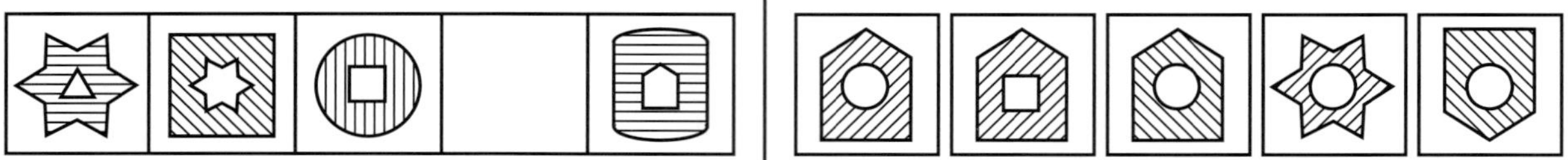

a b c d e

7)

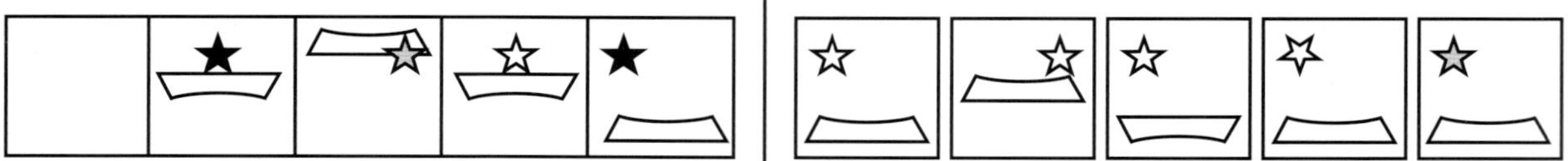

a b c d e

8)

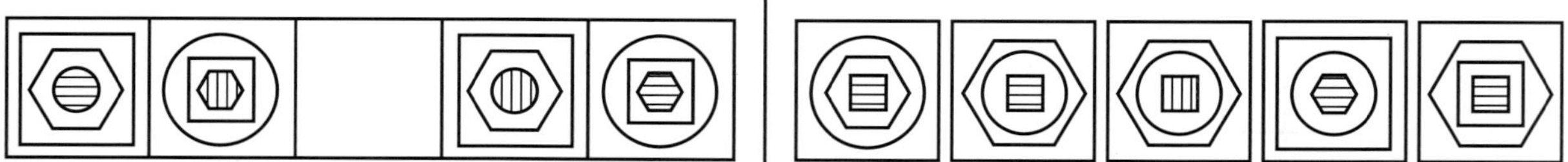

a b c d e

9)

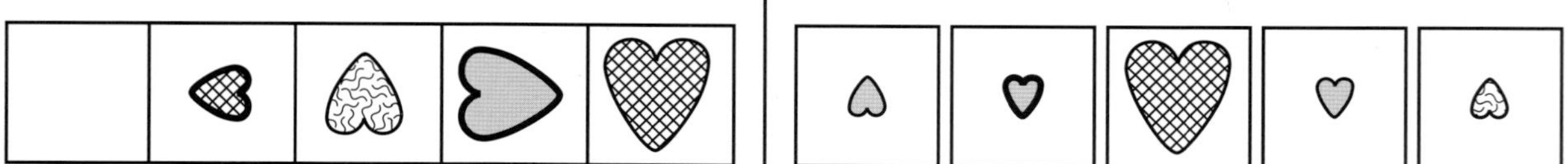

a b c d e

Score

Section B

In the big square on the left of each line below, one of the small squares has been left empty. One of the five figures on the right should fill the empty square. Find this figure.

Example

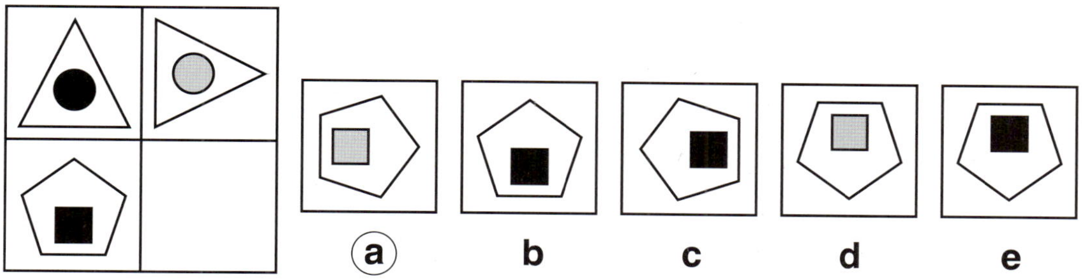

Now do the questions below. Circle the correct answer.

1)

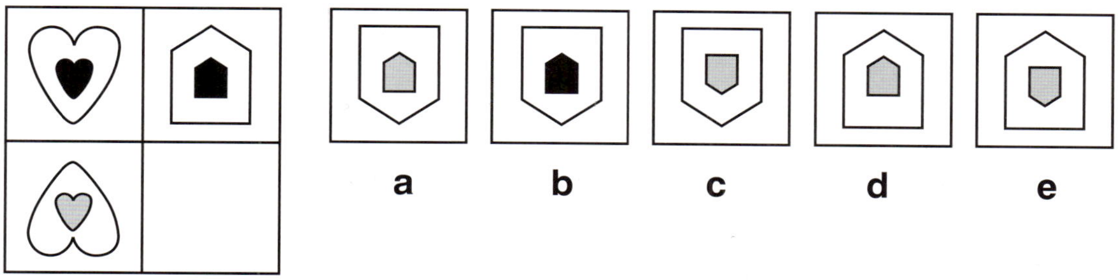

2)

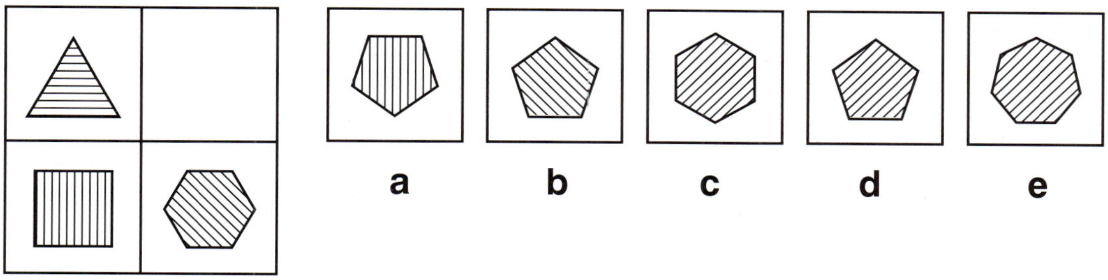

3)

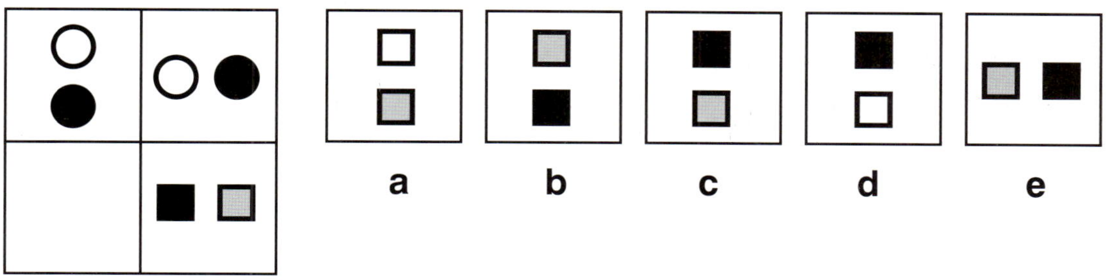

4) 

a **b** **c** **d** **e**

5) 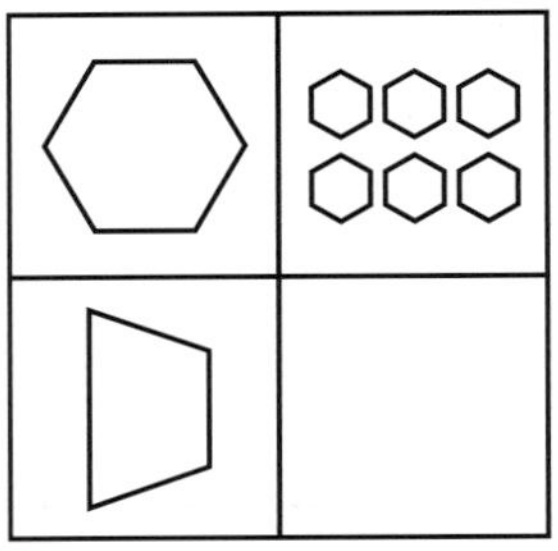

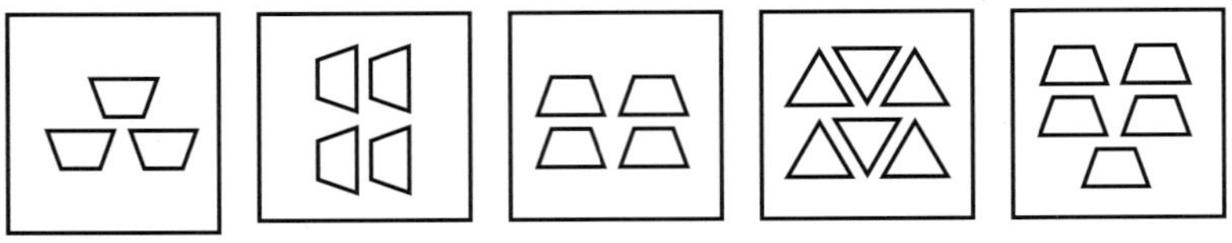

a **b** **c** **d** **e**

6) 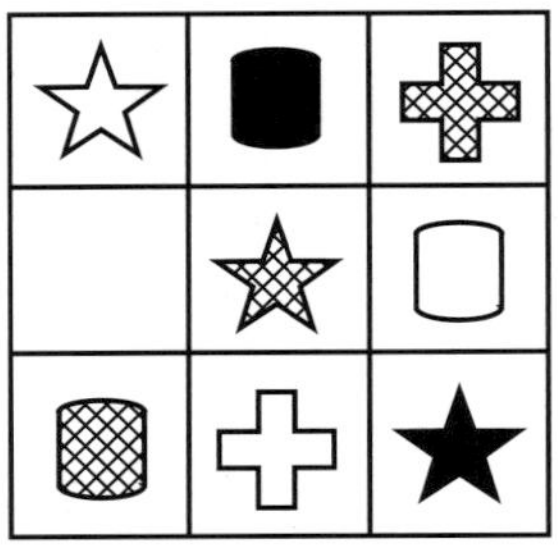

a **b** **c** **d** **e**

7) 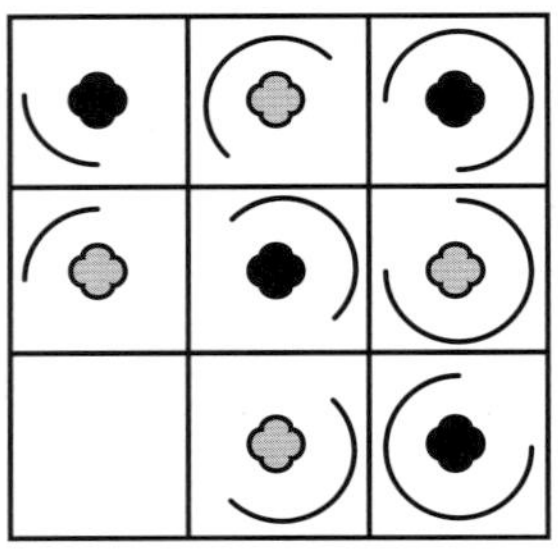

a **b** **c** **d** **e**

8) 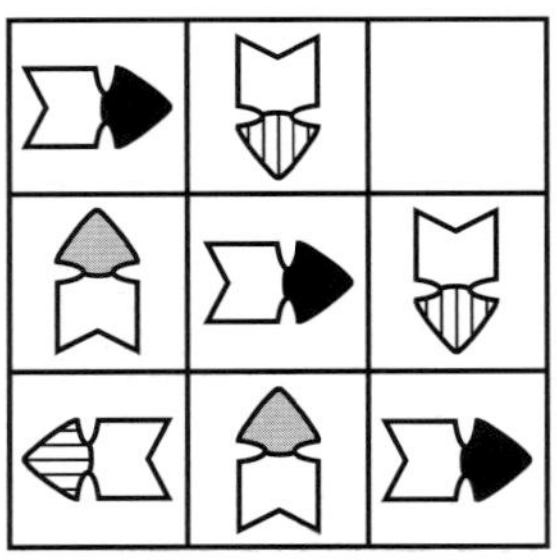

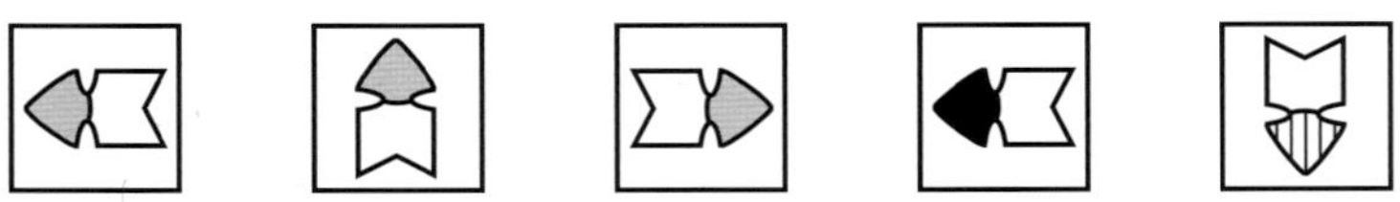

a **b** **c** **d** **e**

Score

Section C

In each of the rows below there are five figures. Find one figure in each row that is **most unlike** the other four.

Example

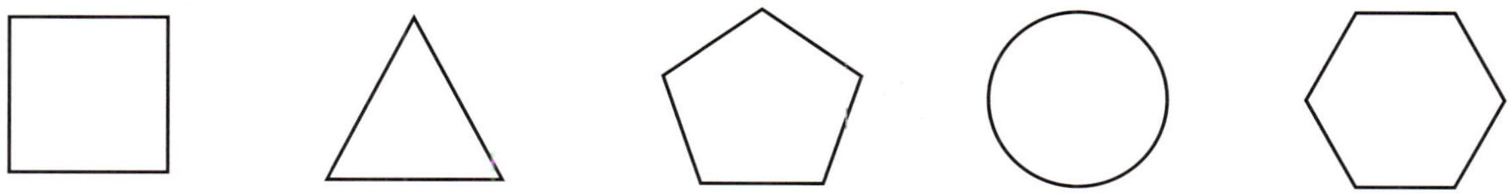

a b c (d) e

Now do the questions below. Circle the correct answer.

1)

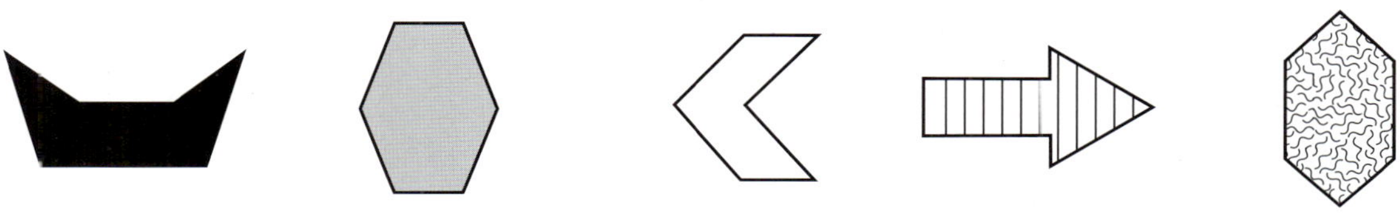

a b c d e

2)

a b c d e

3)

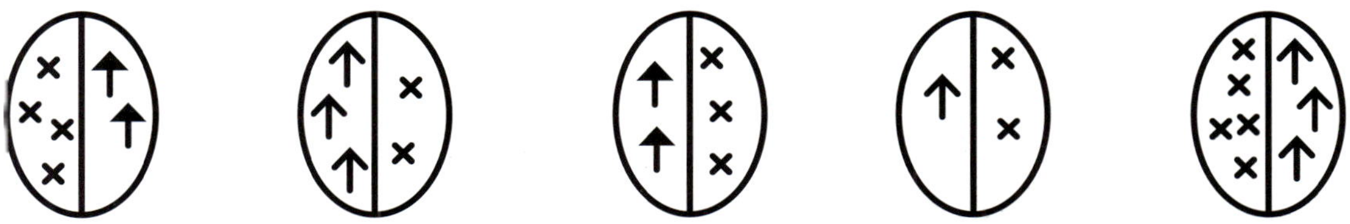

a b c d e

4)

a b c d e

5)

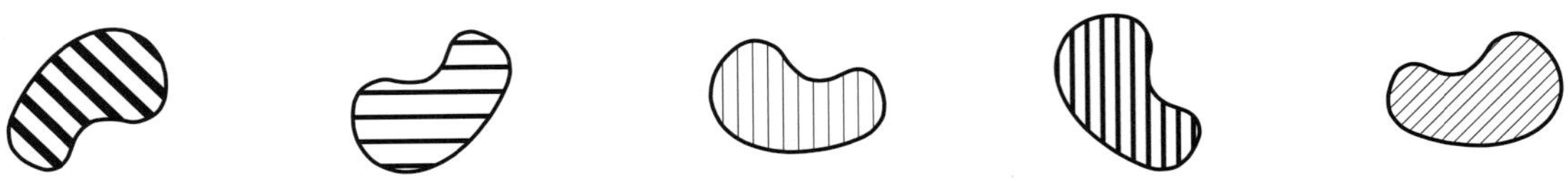

a b c d e

6)

a b c d e

7)

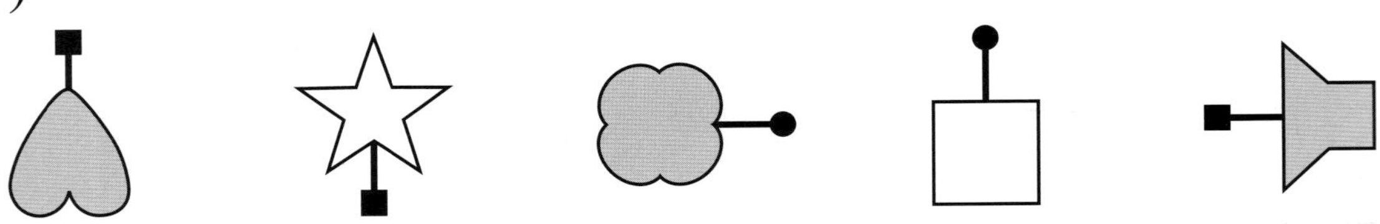

a b c d e

8)

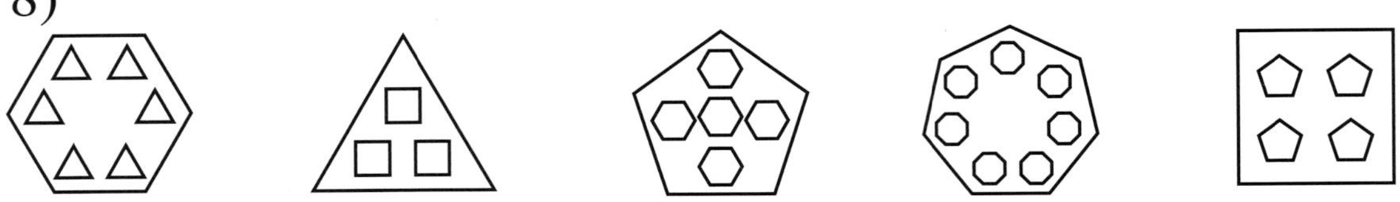

a b c d e

Score

Section D

The following figures correspond to the codes next to them. You must decide how the code letters go with the figures and then find the correct code for the Test Figure.

Example

TEST FIGURE

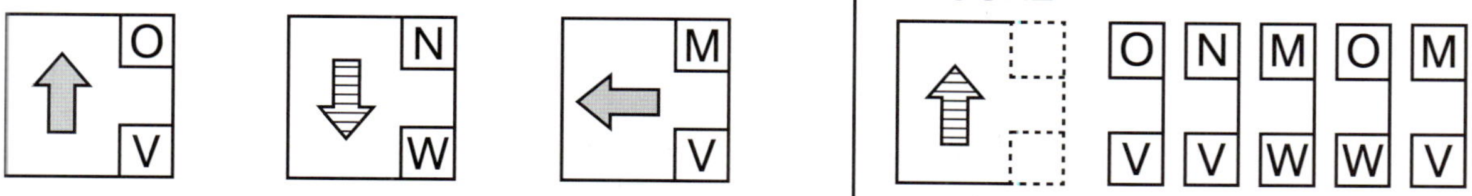

a b (d) c e

Now do the questions below. Circle the correct answer.

1)

TEST FIGURE

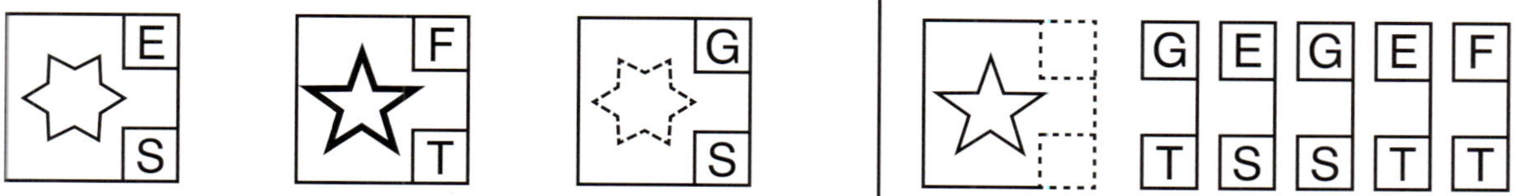

a b c d e

2)

TEST FIGURE

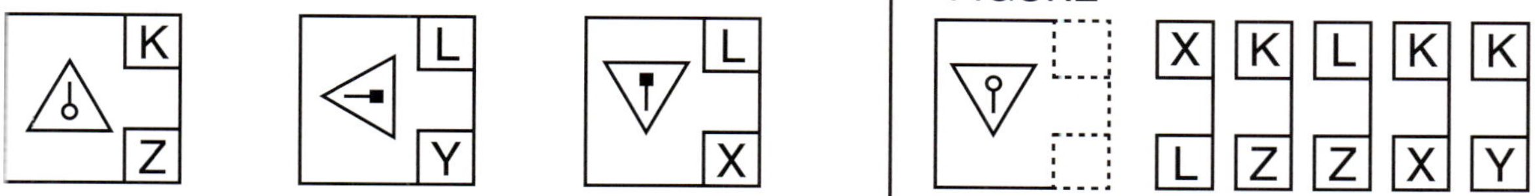

a b c d e

3)

TEST FIGURE

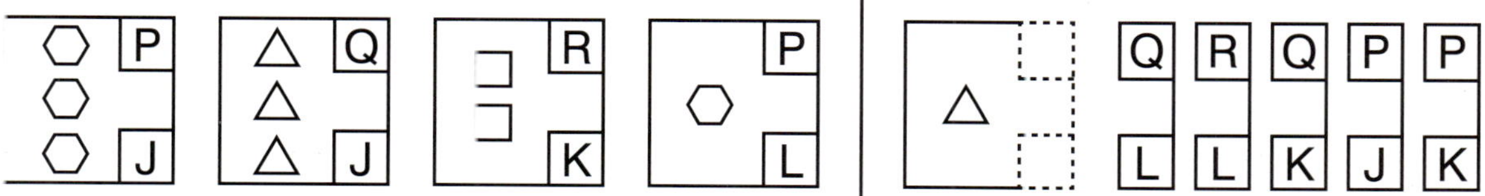

a b c d e

4)

TEST FIGURE

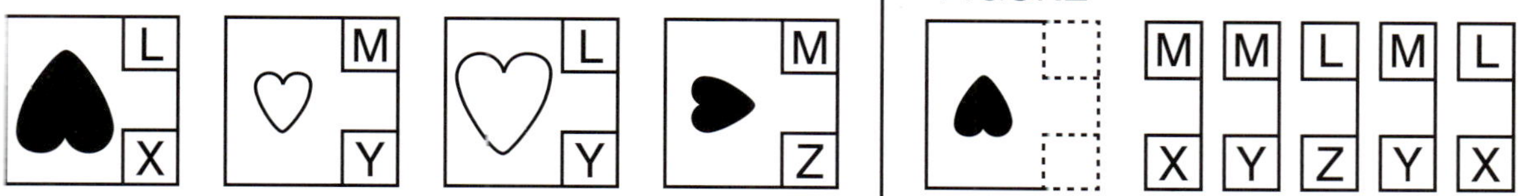

a b c d e

5)

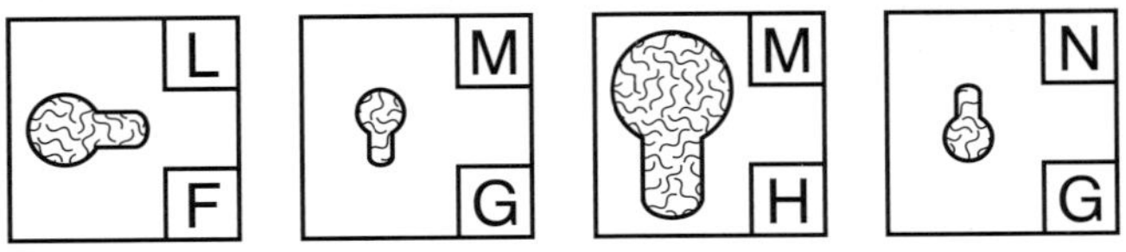

TEST FIGURE

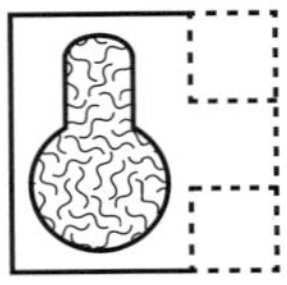

a	b	c	d	e
M	N	N	L	L
F	H	F	H	G

6)

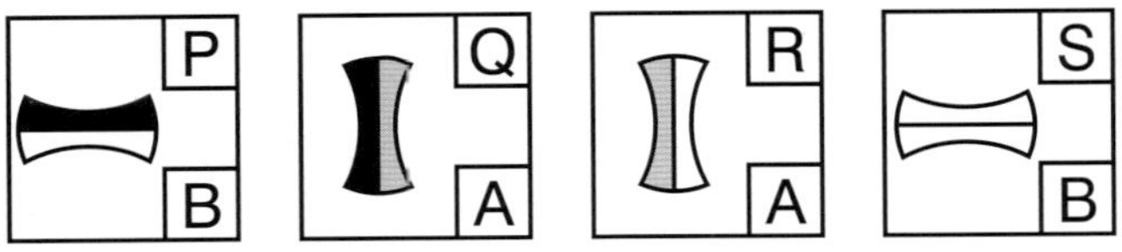

TEST FIGURE

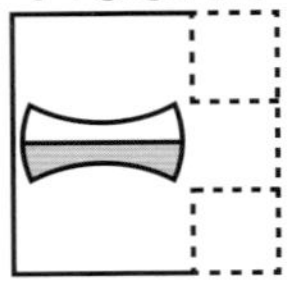

a	b	c	d	e
R	P	Q	S	R
A	B	B	A	B

7)

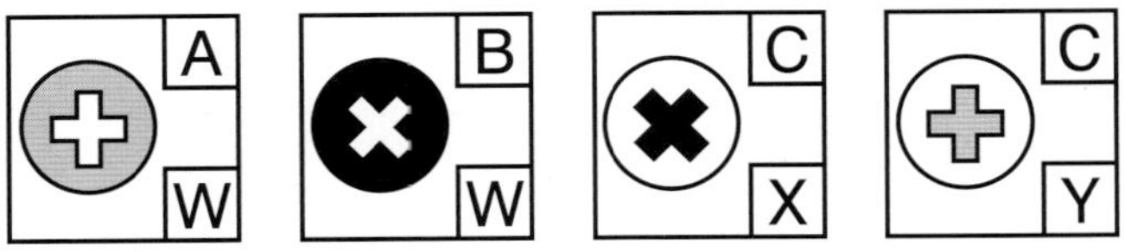

TEST FIGURE

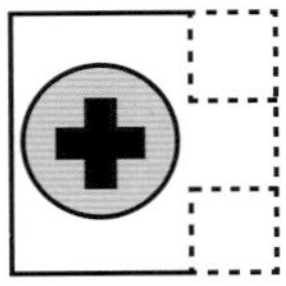

a	b	c	d	e
A	A	C	A	B
W	X	W	Y	X

8)

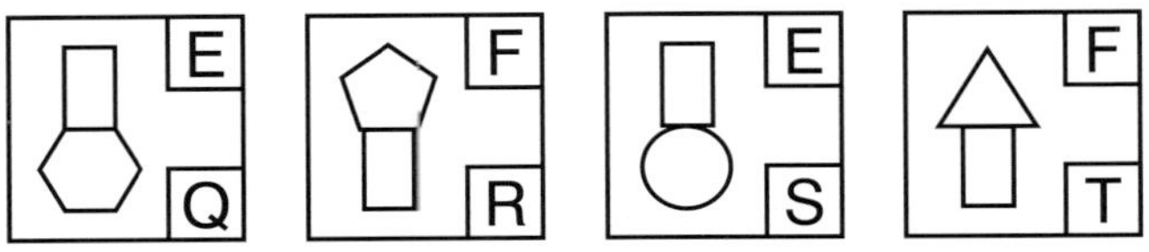

TEST FIGURE

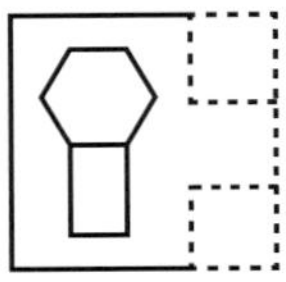

a	b	c	d	e
F	E	F	E	F
S	R	Q	T	R

9)

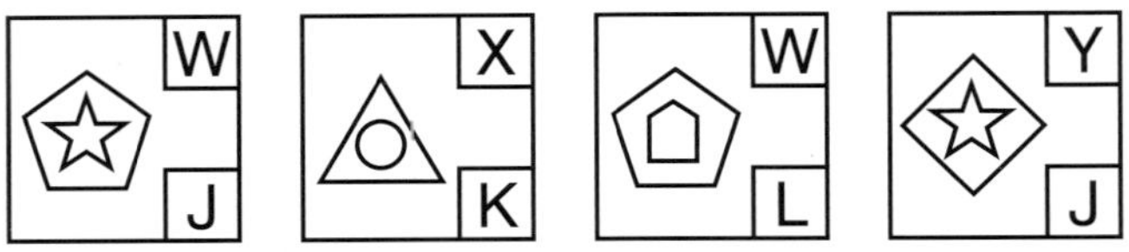

TEST FIGURE

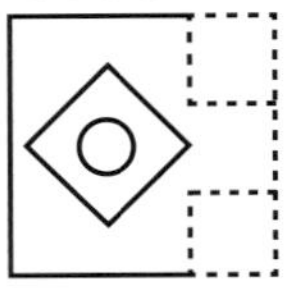

a	b	c	d	e
W	Y	X	Y	X
K	L	L	K	J

10)

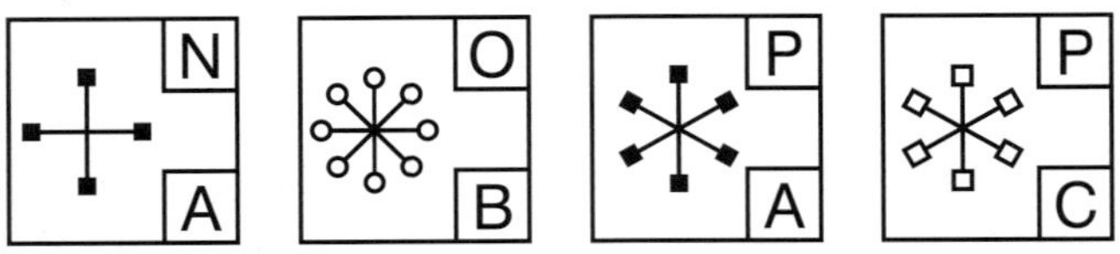

TEST FIGURE

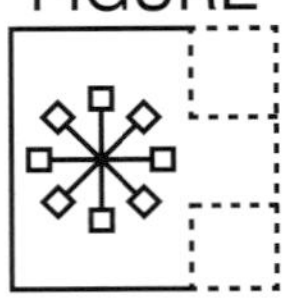

a	b	c	d	e
O	O	N	N	P
C	A	C	B	B

Score

Non-verbal Reasoning Test 2

Section A

On the left of each row are two figures with an arrow between them. Decide how the second figure is related to the first. After these there is a third figure, then an arrow and then five more figures. Decide which of the five figures goes with the third figure to make a pair like the two figures on the left.

Example

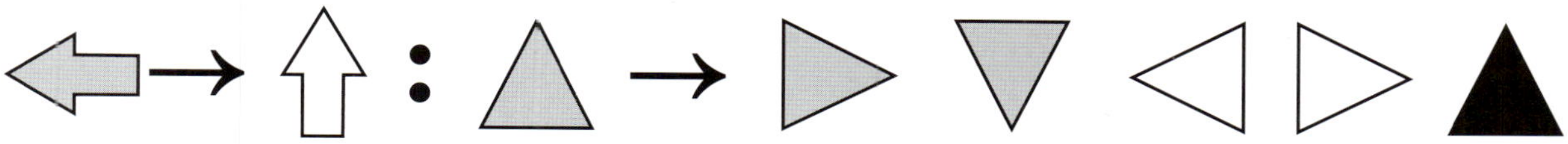

a b c (d) e

Now do the questions below. Circle the correct answer.

1)

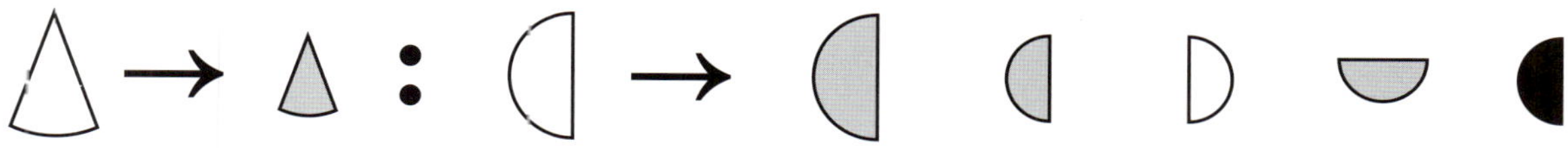

a b c d e

2)

a b c d e

3)

a b c d e

4)

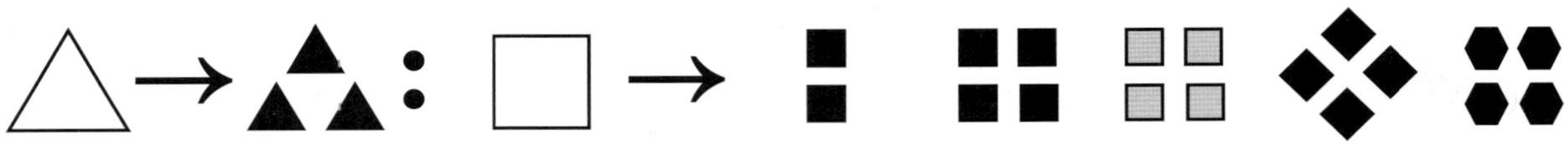

a b c d e

5)

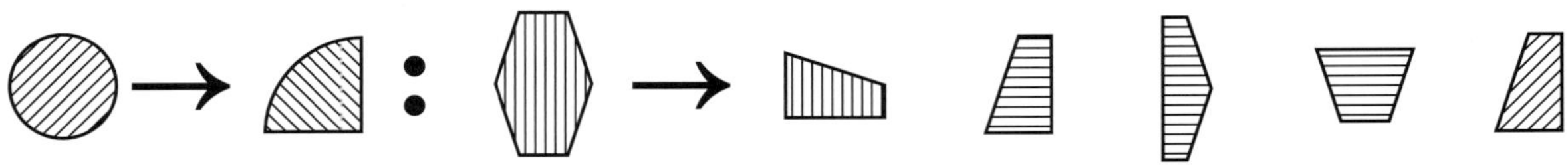

a b c d e

6)

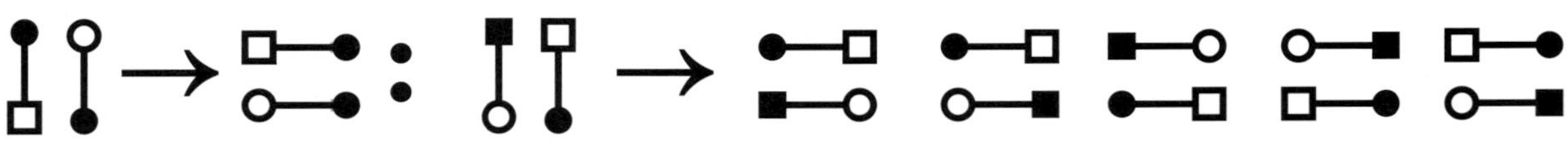

a b c d e

7)

a b c d e

8)

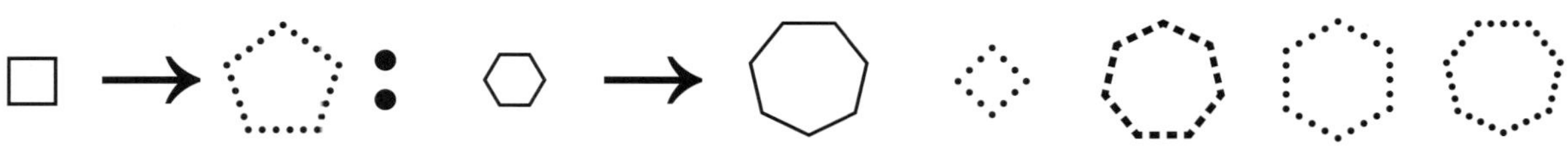

a b c d e

Score

Section B

In each of the rows below there are five figures. Find one figure in each row that is **most unlike** the other four.

Example

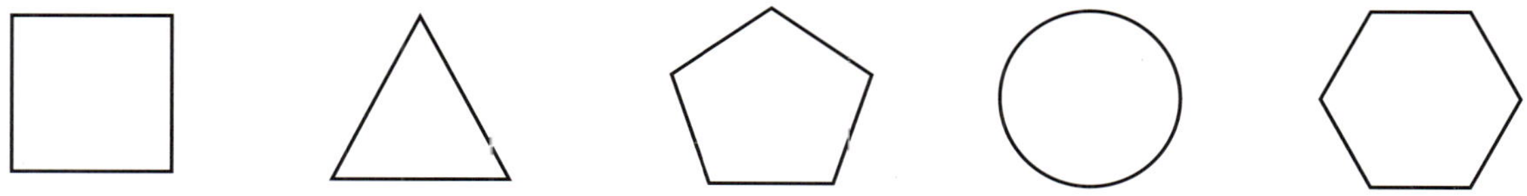

a b c d e

Now do the questions below. Circle the correct answer.

1)

a b c d e

2)

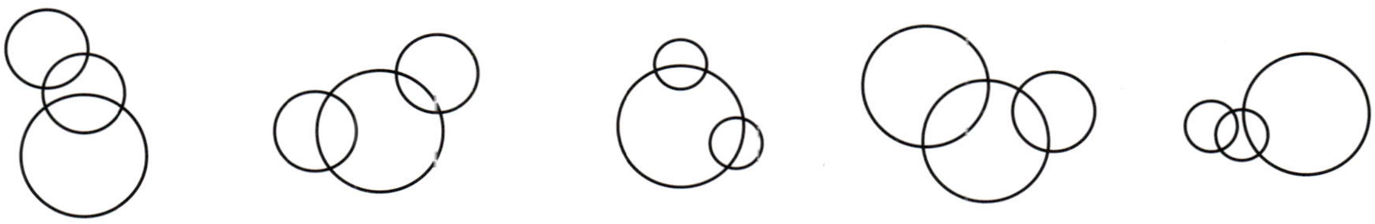

a b c d e

3)

a b c d e

4)

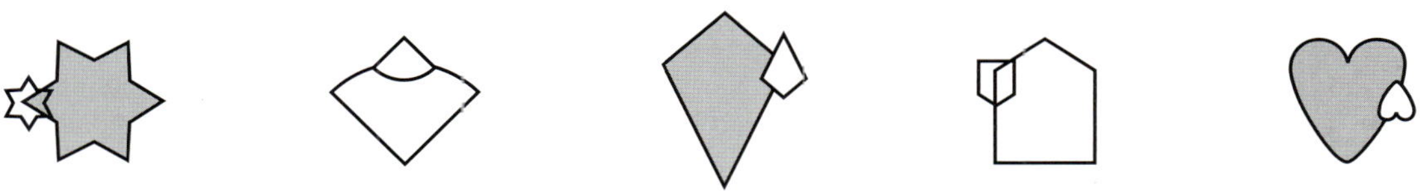

a b c d e

5)

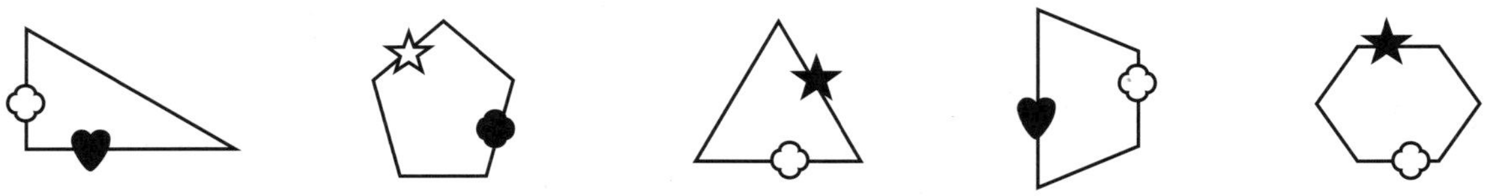

a **b** **c** **d** **e**

6)

a **b** **c** **d** **e**

7)

a **b** **c** **d** **e**

8)

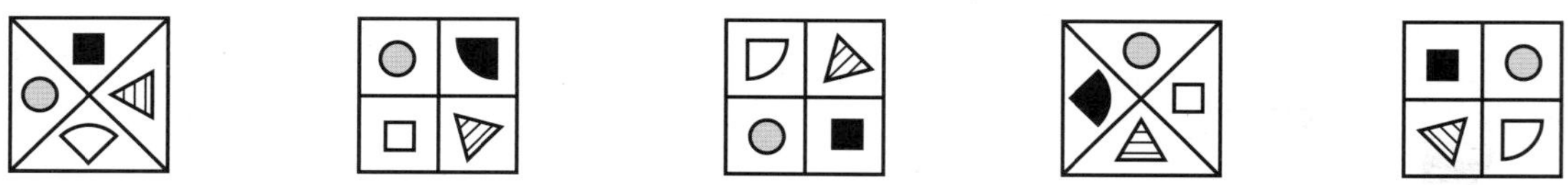

a **b** **c** **d** **e**

9)

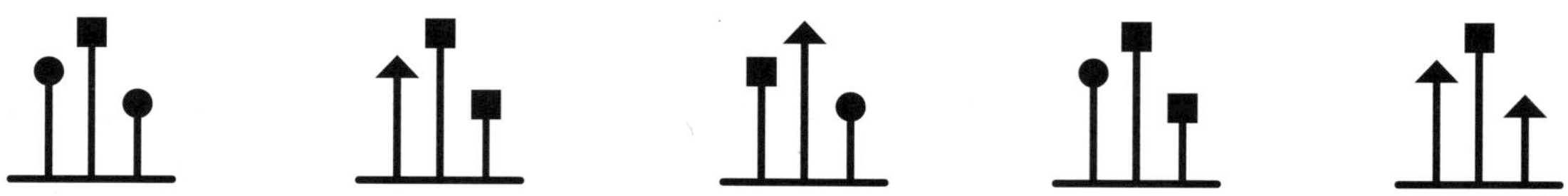

a **b** **c** **d** **e**

Score

Section C

The following figures correspond to the codes next to them. You must decide how the code letters go with the figures and then find the correct code for the Test Figure.

Example

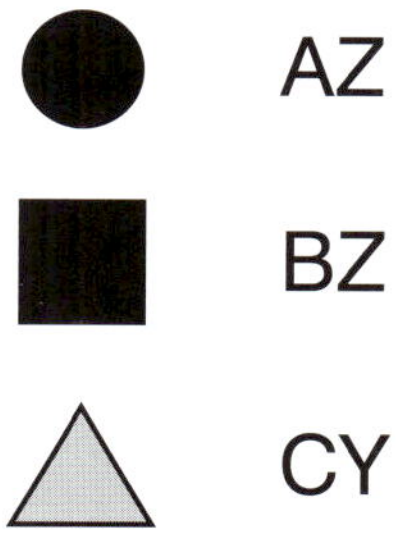

TEST FIGURE

CZ	BY	AY	BZ	AZ
a	b	c	d	e

Now do the questions below. Circle the correct answer.

1)

TEST FIGURE

TC	SD	UC	TD	UD
a	b	c	d	e

2)

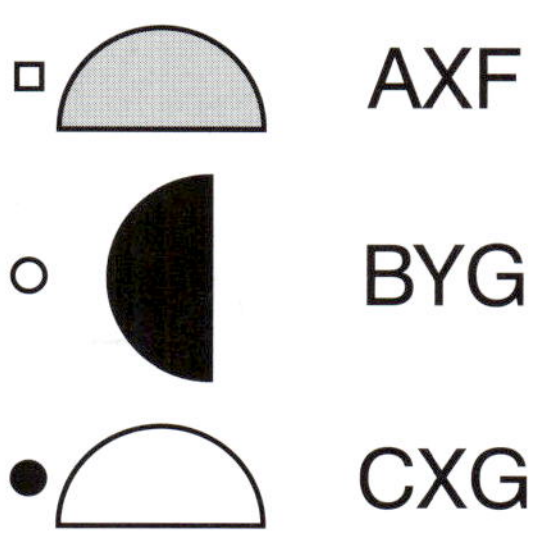

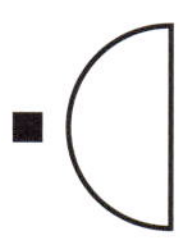

TEST FIGURE

CXF	AYF	CYF	CYG	BXF
a	b	c	d	e

3)

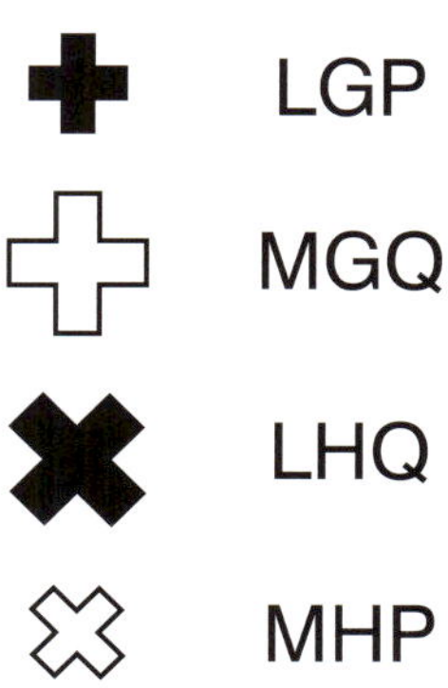

TEST FIGURE

MGP	MHQ	LHP	LGQ	MGQ
a	b	c	d	e

4)

LRP

LSQ

MRQ

TEST FIGURE

LSP	MSP	MRP	MSQ	LRQ
a	b	c	d	e

5)

PIV

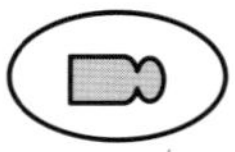
PJW

QKV

TEST FIGURE

QIW	QKV	PKW	PIW	QJW
a	b	c	d	e

6)

XAQ

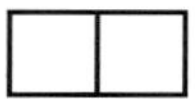
YAR

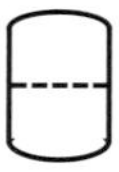
ZBQ

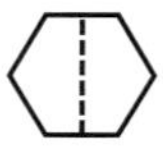
ZAS

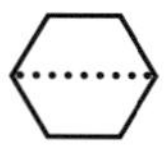
TEST FIGURE

YBS	XBQ	XBS	XAR	ZBS
a	b	c	d	e

7)

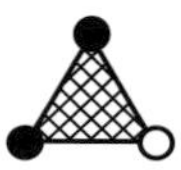
RMX

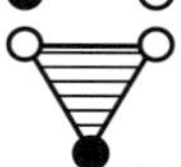
SNY

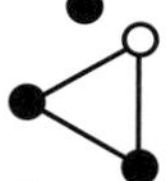
ROZ

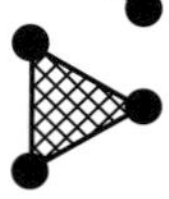
TPX

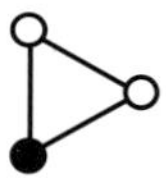
TEST FIGURE

RPZ	SOZ	TNZ	SPY	SPZ
a	b	c	d	e

8)

NKDR

OLER

NLFS

OMDT

TEST FIGURE

OKFR	NKFT	OMFT	OKFT	OKDS
a	b	c	d	e

Score

Section D

On the left of each of the rows below there are two figures that are alike. On the right there are five more figures. Find which one of these five is **most like** the two figures on the left.

Example

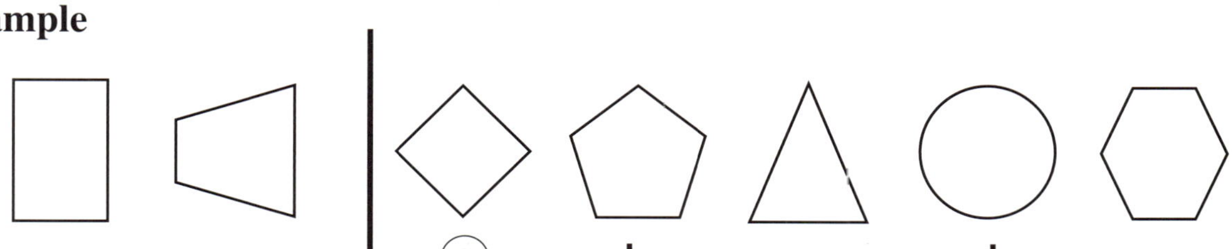

a b c d e

Now do the questions below. Circle the correct answer.

1)

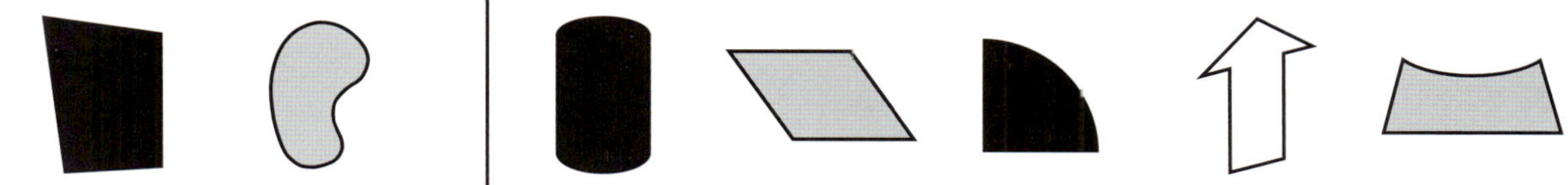

a b c d e

2)

a b c d e

3)

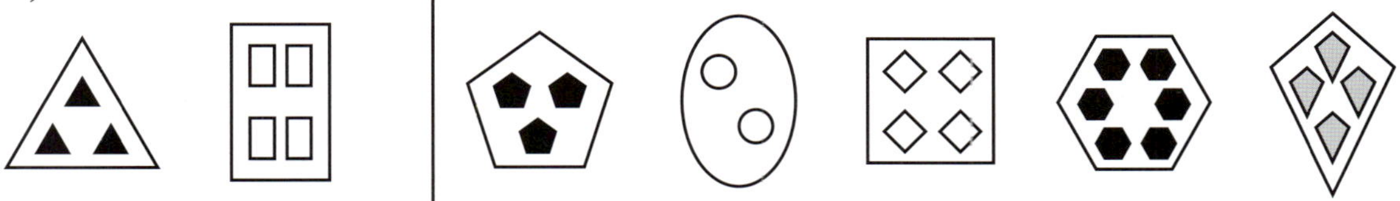

a b c d e

4)

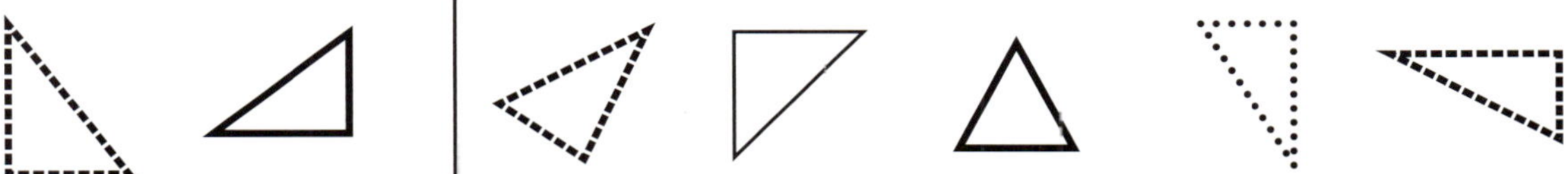

a b c d e

5)

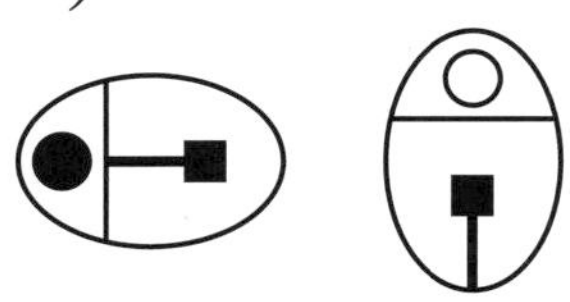

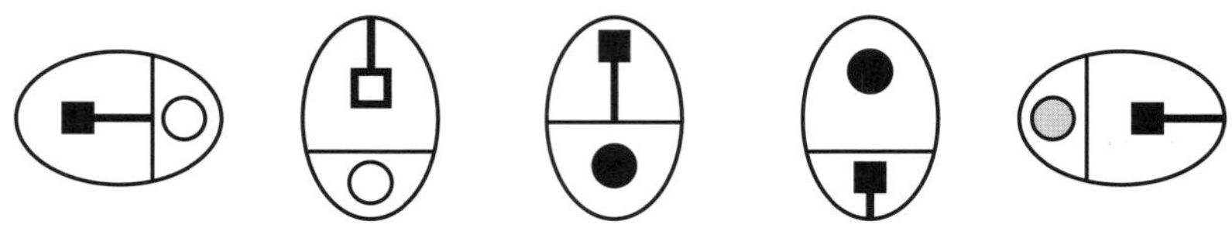

a b c d e

6)

a b c d e

7)

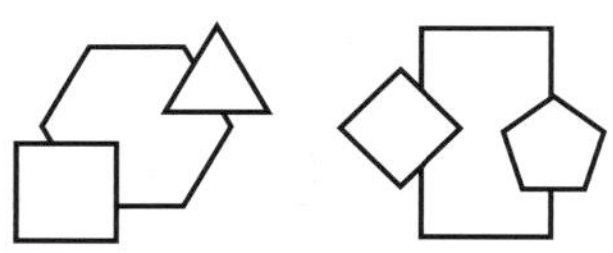

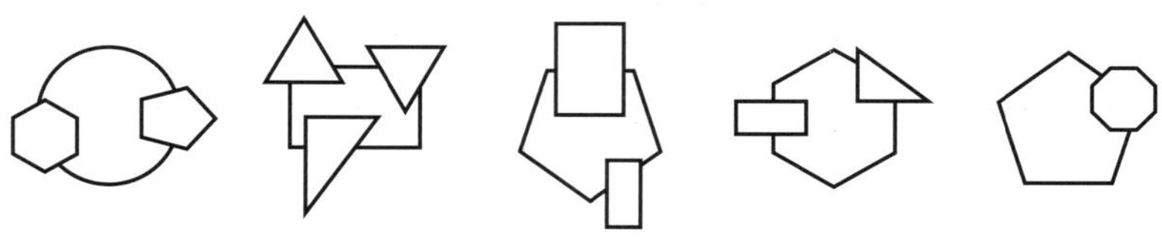

a b c d e

8)

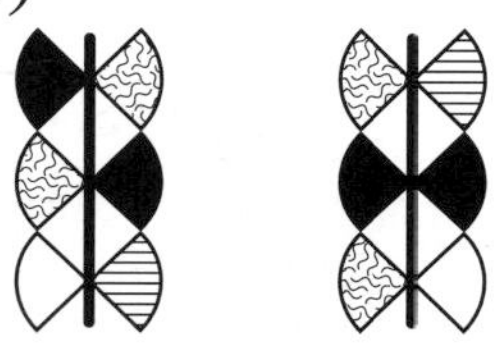

a b c d e

9)

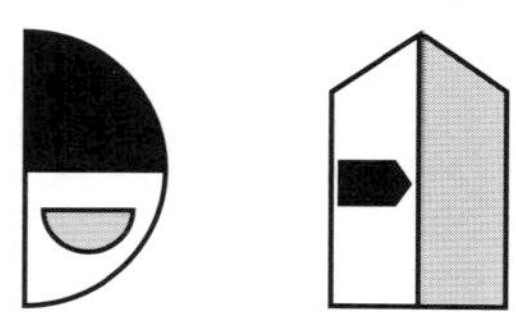

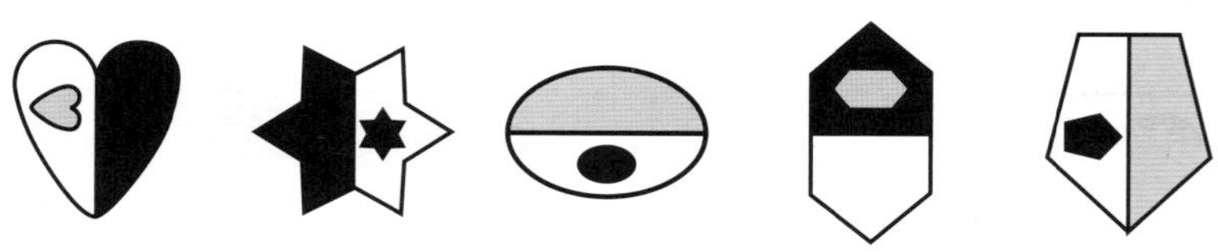

a b c d e

10)

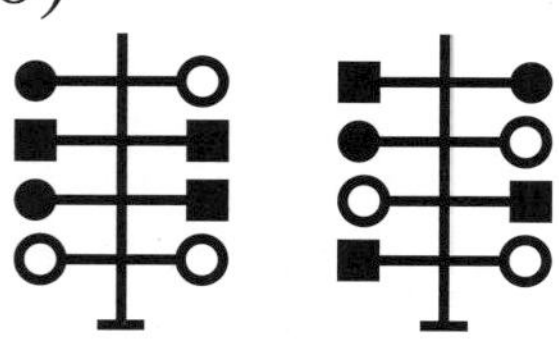

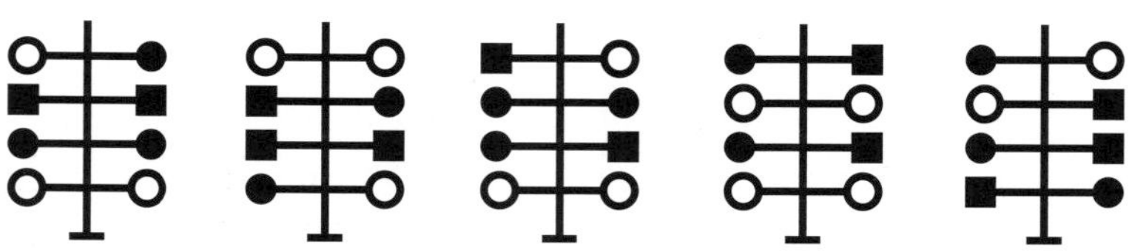

a b c d e

Score

Non-verbal Reasoning Test 3

Section A

The following figures correspond to the codes next to them. You must decide how the code letters go with the figures and then find the correct code for the Test Figure.

Example

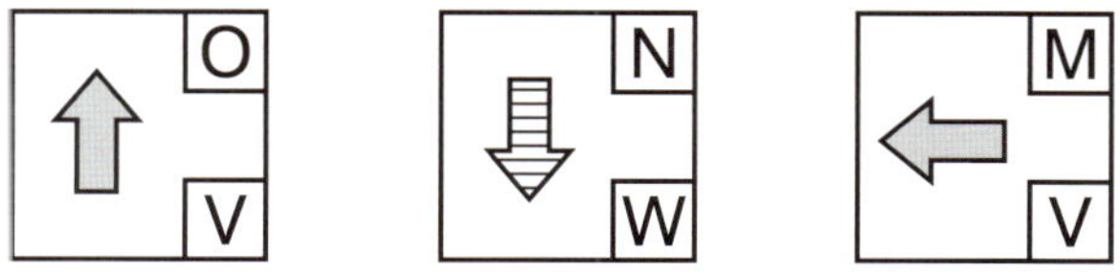

TEST FIGURE

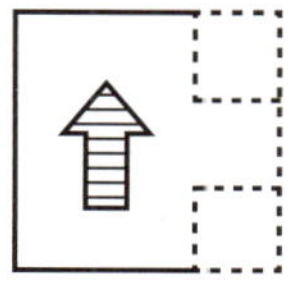

a	b	c	d	e
O	N	M	O	M
V	V	W	W	V

(d is circled)

Now do the questions below. Circle the correct answer.

1)

TEST FIGURE

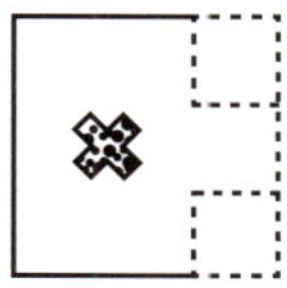

a	b	c	d	e
M	N	O	M	O
J	J	J	I	I

2)

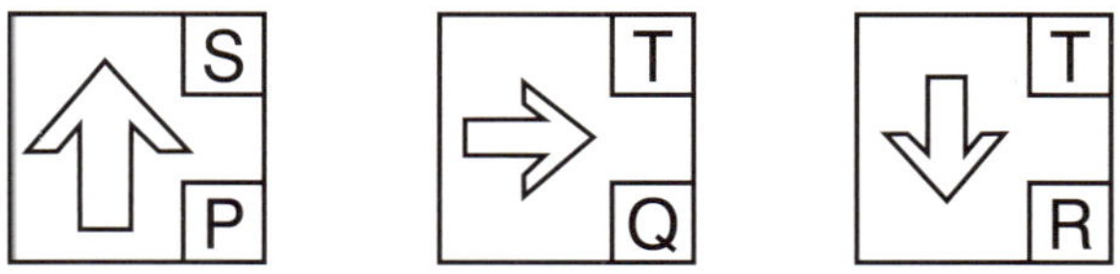

TEST FIGURE

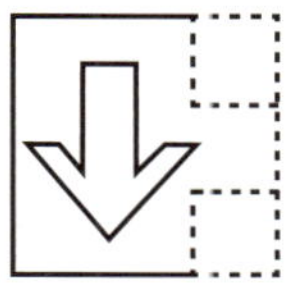

a	b	c	d	e
S	T	S	S	T
Q	P	R	P	R

3)

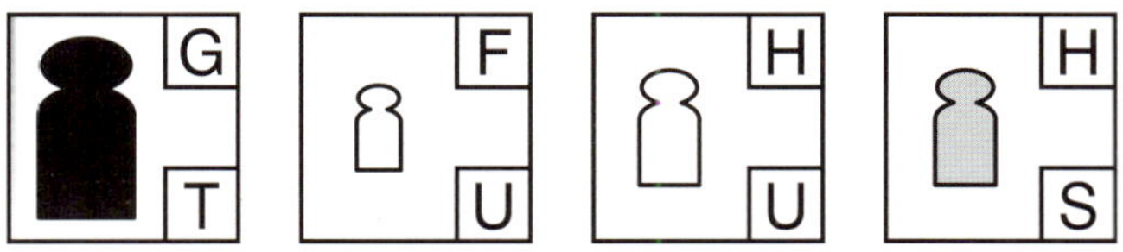

TEST FIGURE

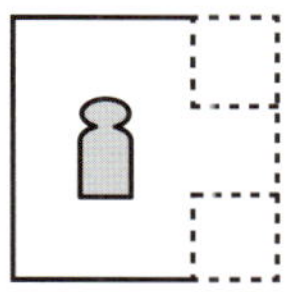

a	b	c	d	e
F	G	F	F	G
U	S	T	S	U

4)

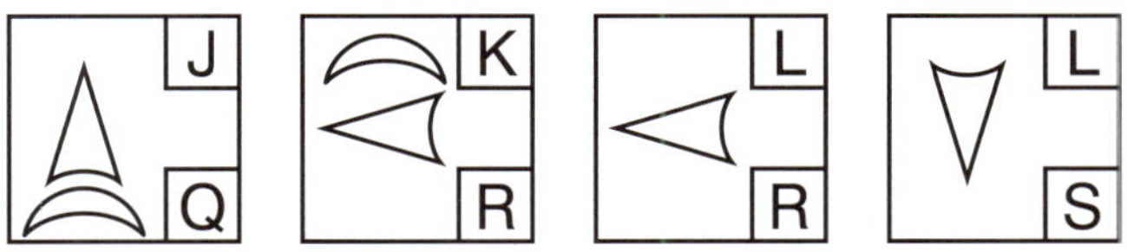

TEST FIGURE

a	b	c	d	e
J	L	K	J	K
Q	Q	S	R	Q

5)

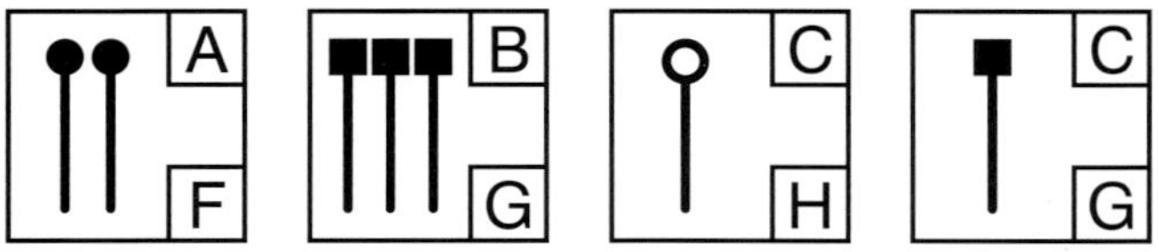

TEST FIGURE

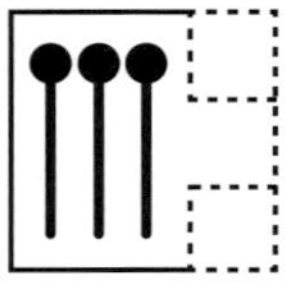

a	b	c	d	e
A	C	B	A	B
H	F	F	G	H

6)

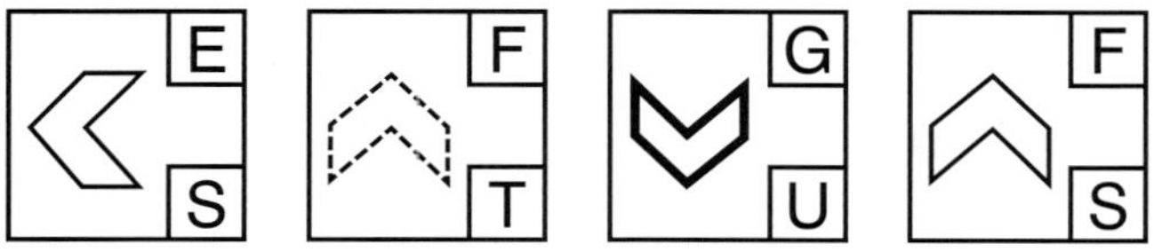

TEST FIGURE

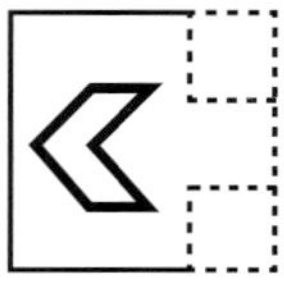

a	b	c	d	e
E	F	E	G	G
U	U	T	T	S

7)

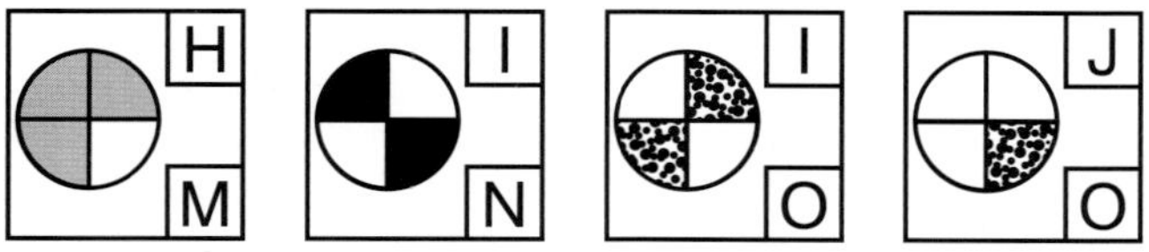

TEST FIGURE

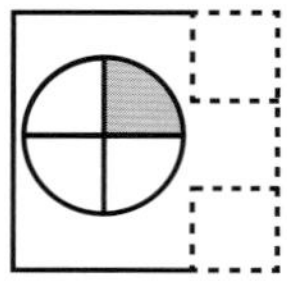

a	b	c	d	e
I	J	J	H	H
M	M	N	N	O

8)

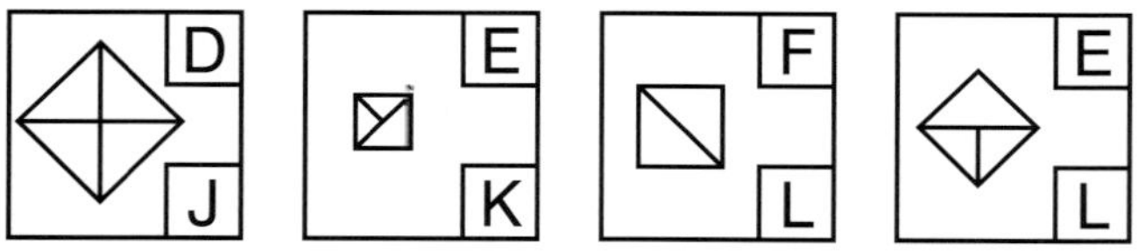

TEST FIGURE

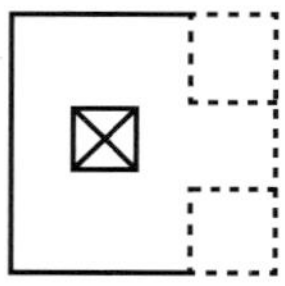

a	b	c	d	e
D	F	E	D	F
L	K	J	K	J

9)

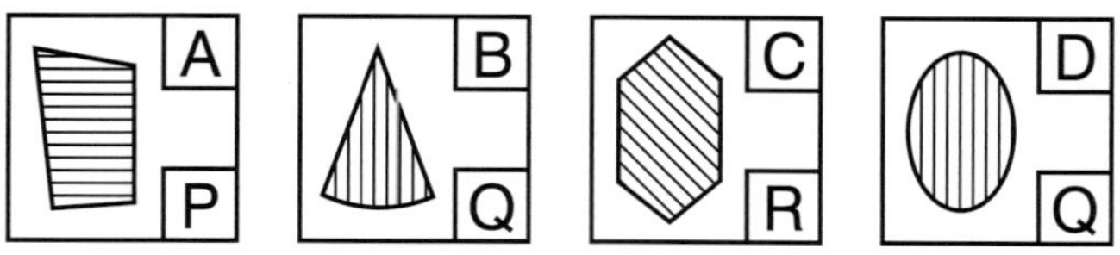

TEST FIGURE

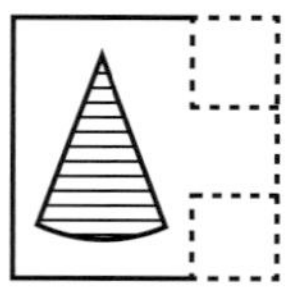

a	b	c	d	e
C	B	D	B	A
P	P	P	R	Q

Score

Section B

In the big square on the left of each line below, one of the small squares has been left empty. One of the five figures on the right should fill the empty square. Find this figure.

Example

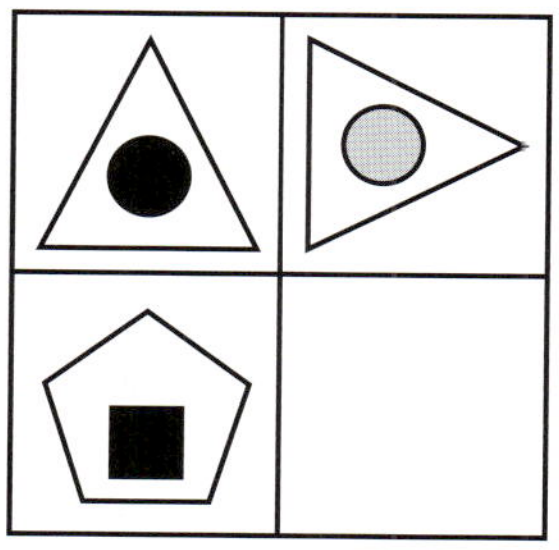

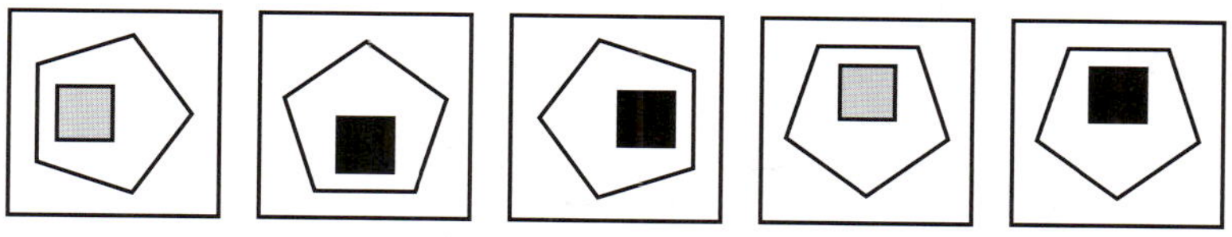

(a) b c d e

Now do the questions below. Circle the correct answer.

1)

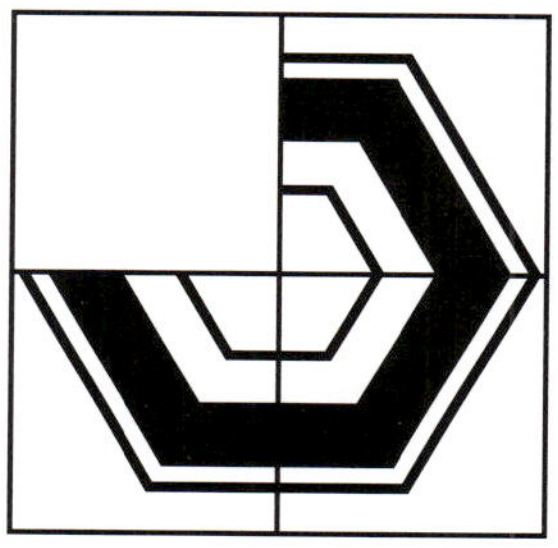

a b c d e

2)

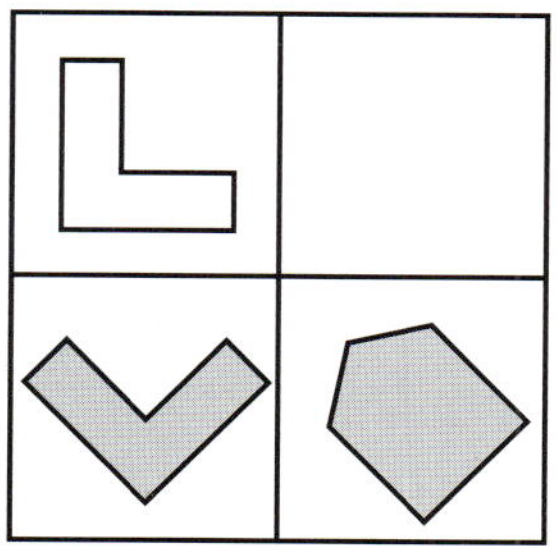

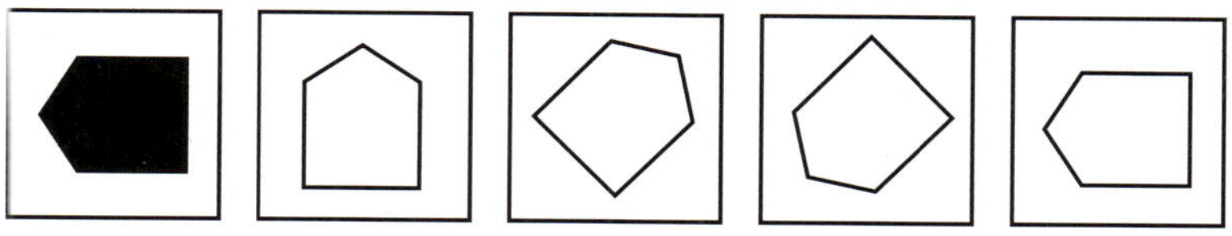

a b c d e

3)

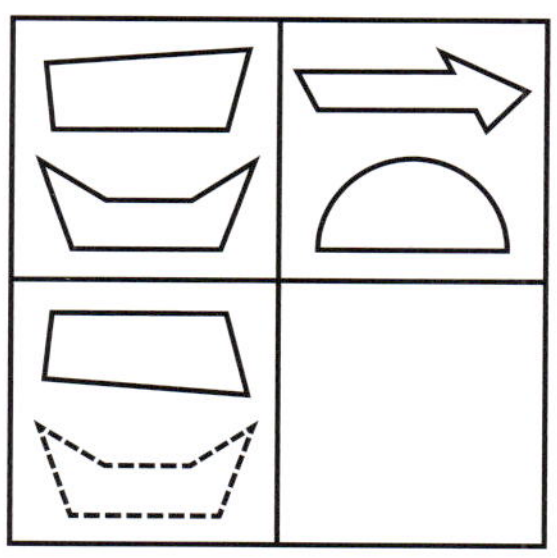

a b c d e

4) 

a b c d e

5) 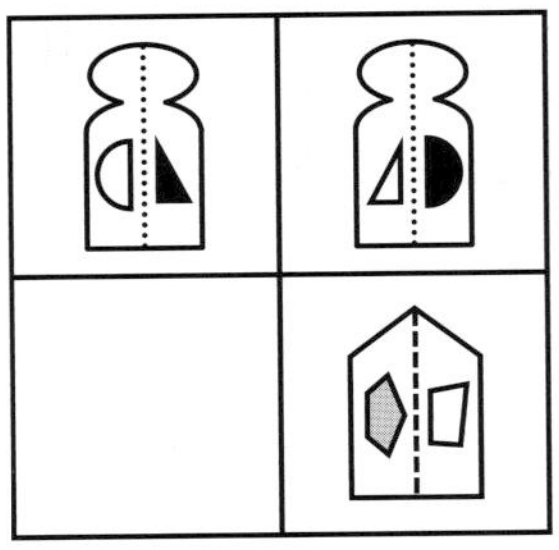

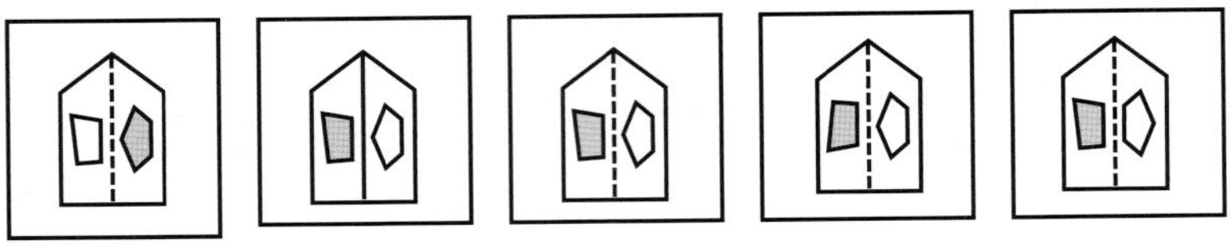

a b c d e

6) 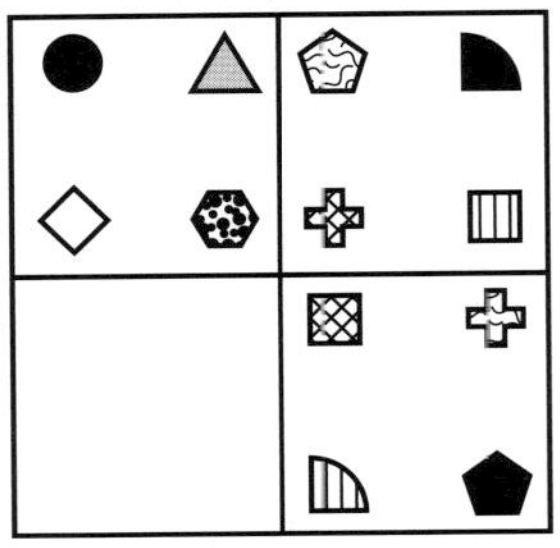

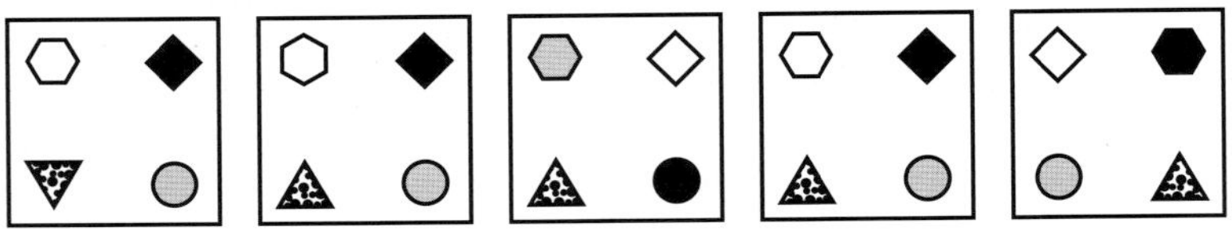

a b c d e

7) 

a b c d e

8) 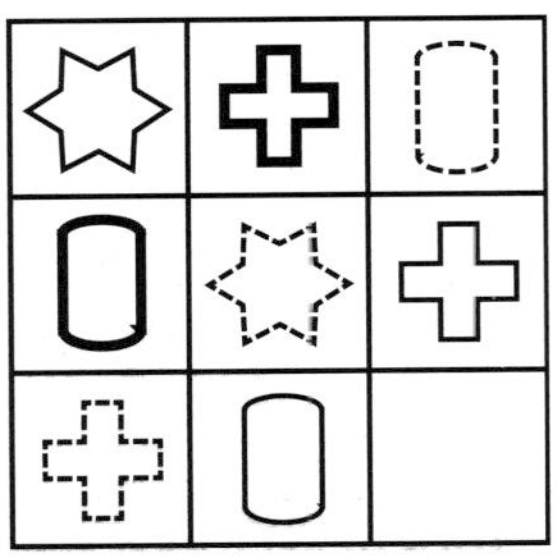

a b c d e

Score

Section C

To the left of each of the lines below there are five squares arranged in order. One of these squares has been left empty. Find which one of the five squares on the right should take the place of the empty square.

Example

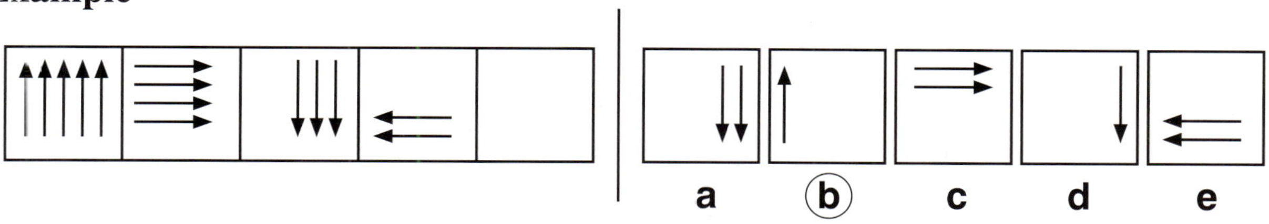

Now do the questions below. Circle the correct answer.

1)

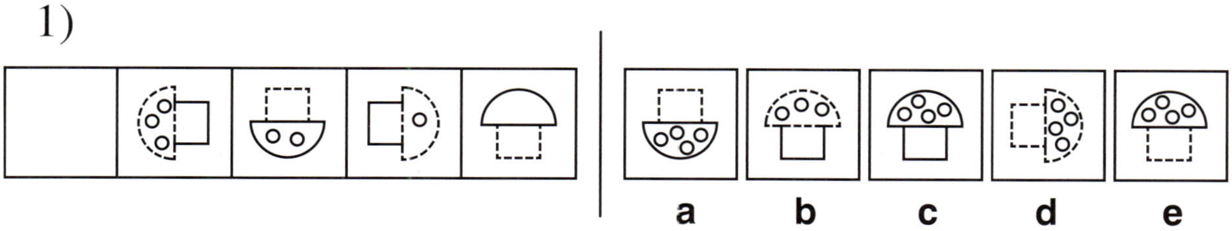

2)

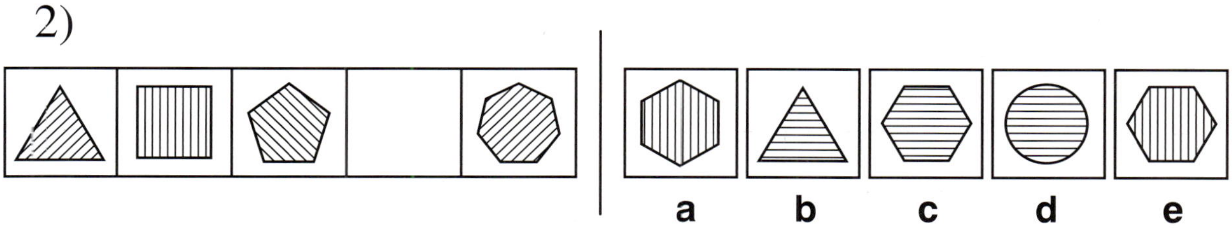

3)

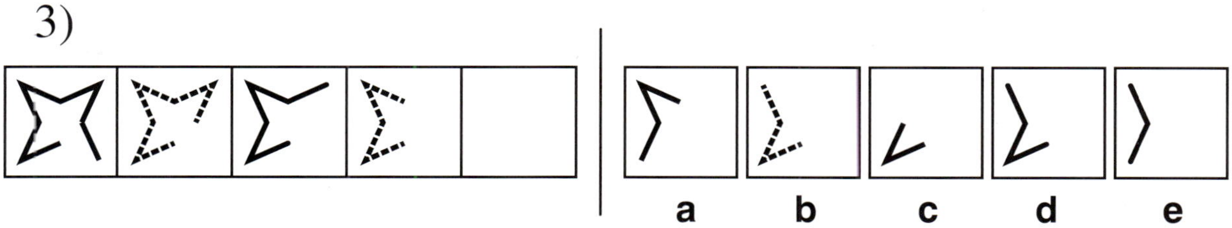

4)

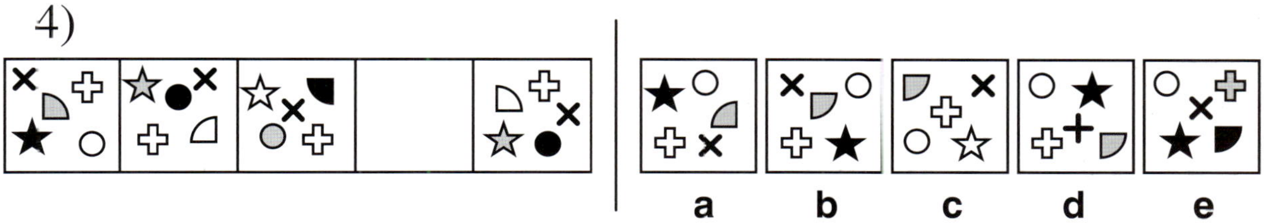

5)

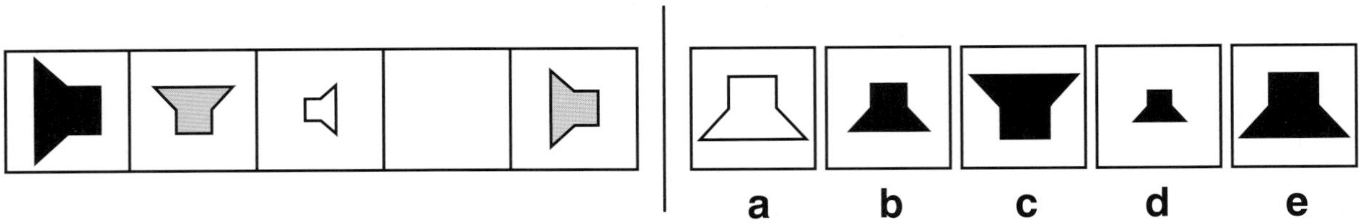

a b c d e

6)

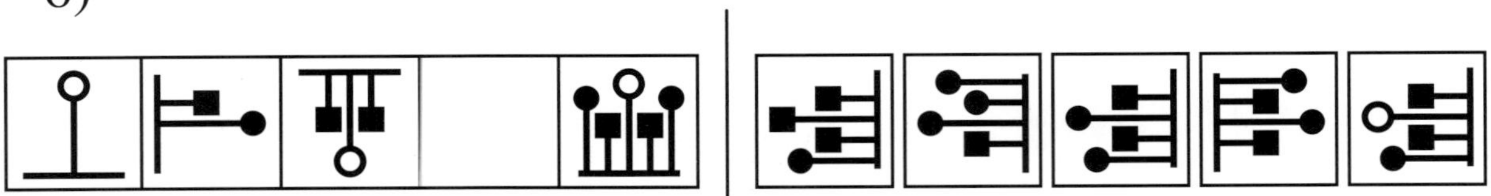

a b c d e

7)

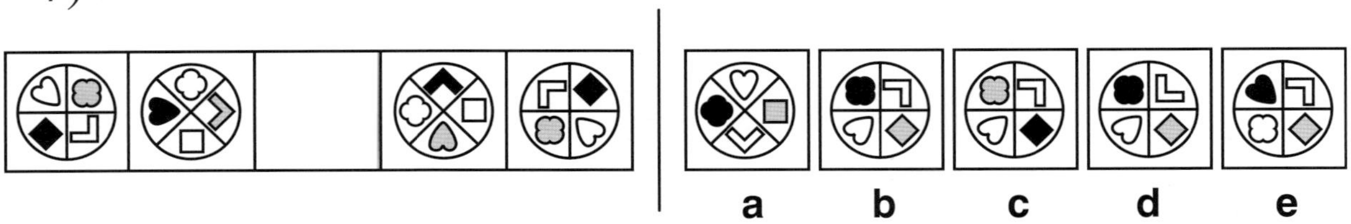

a b c d e

8)

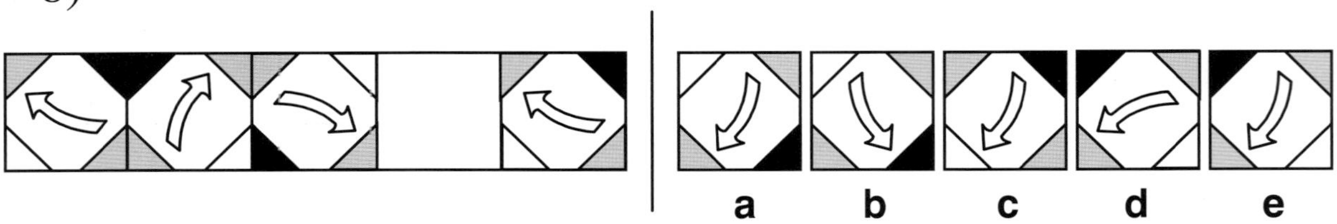

a b c d e

9)

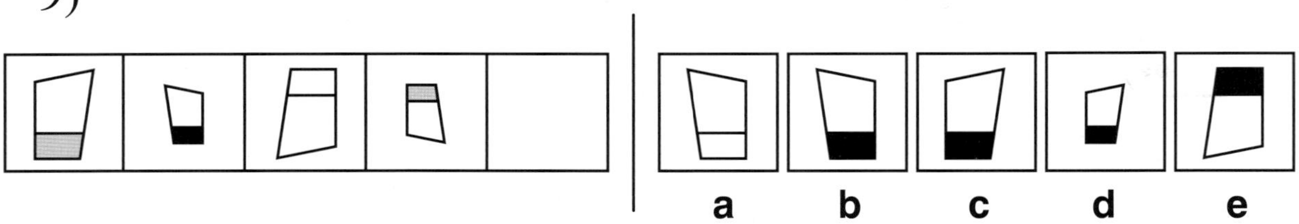

a b c d e

10)

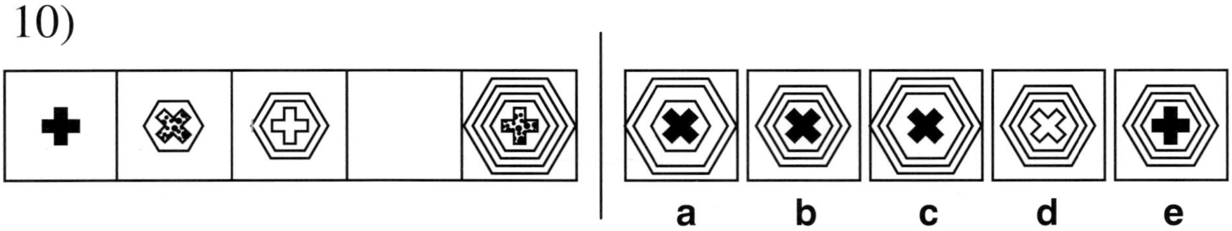

a b c d e

Score

Section D

In each of the rows below there are five figures. Find one figure in each row that is **most unlike** the other four.

Example

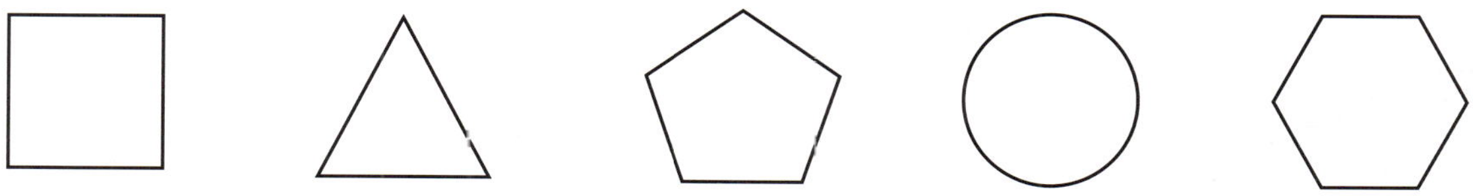

a b c (d) e

Now do the questions below. Circle the correct answer.

1)

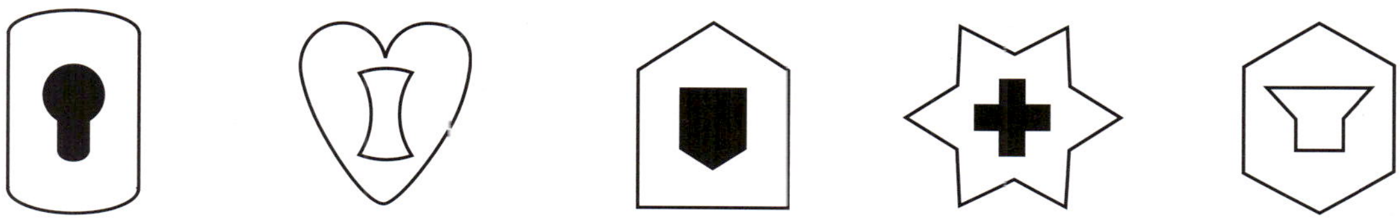

a b c d e

2)

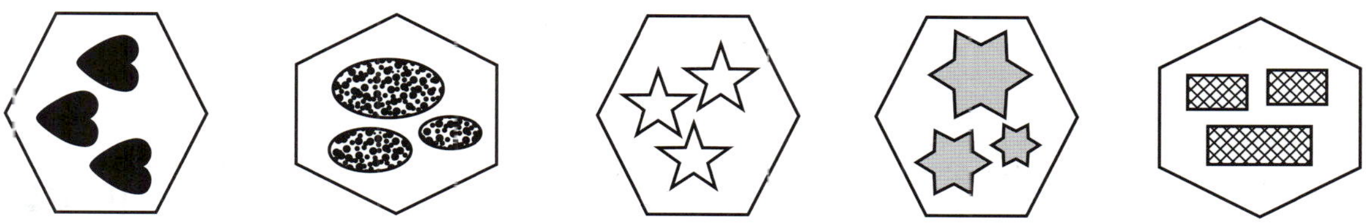

a b c d e

3)

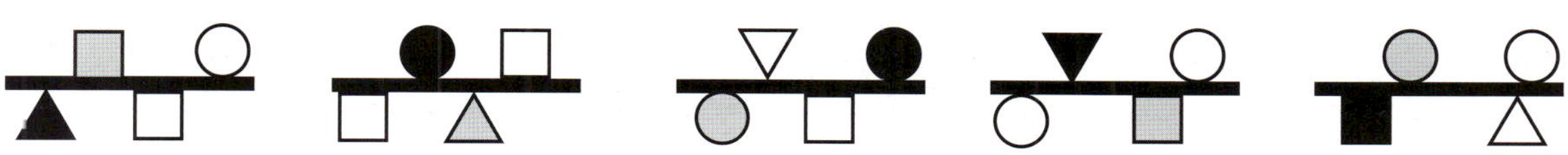

a b c d e

4)

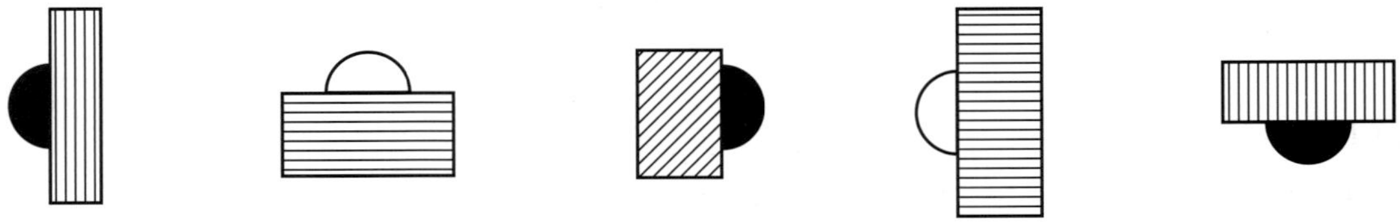

a b c d e

5)

a b c d e

6)

a b c d e

7)

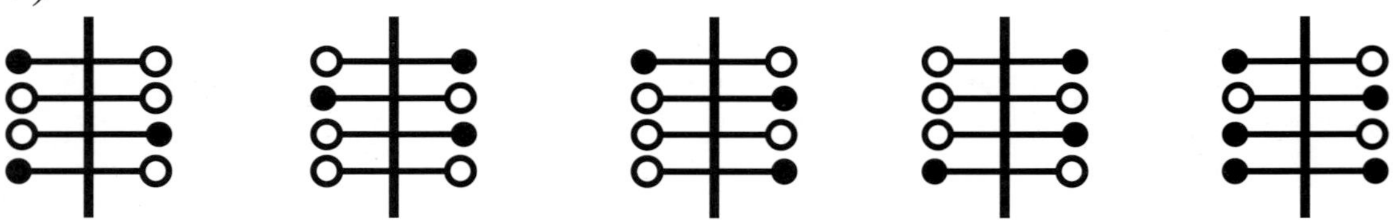

a b c d e

8)

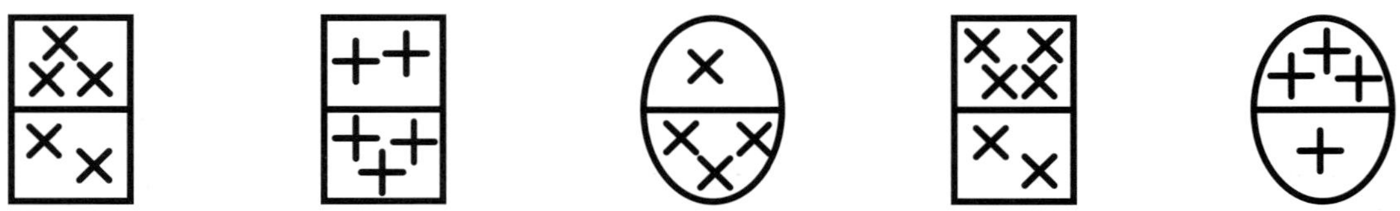

a b c d e

Score

Non-verbal Reasoning Test 4

Section A

On the left of each row are two figures with an arrow between them. Decide how the second figure is related to the first. After these there is a third figure, then an arrow and then five more figures. Decide which of the five figures goes with the third figure to make a pair like the two figures on the left.

Example

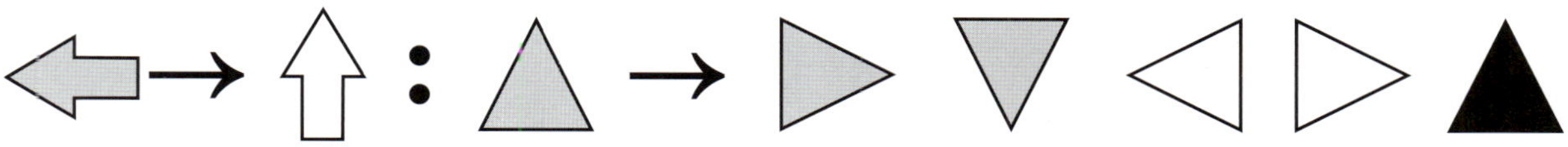

a b c (d) e

Now do the questions below. Circle the correct answer.

1)

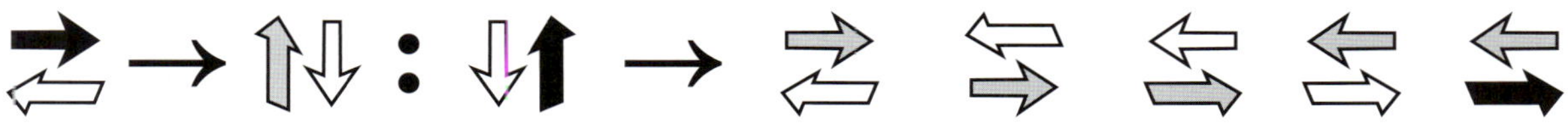

a b c d e

2)

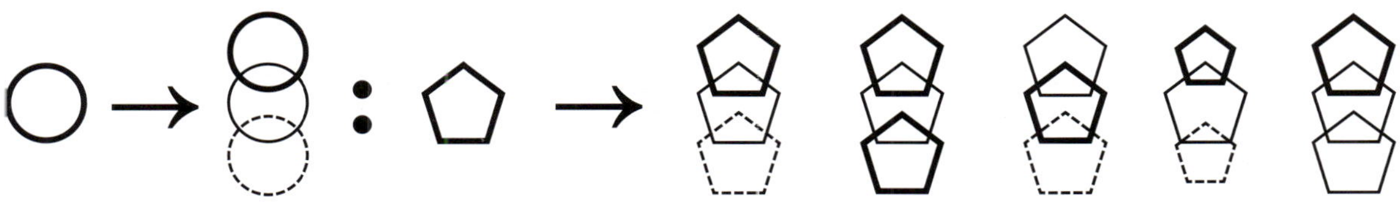

a b c d e

3)

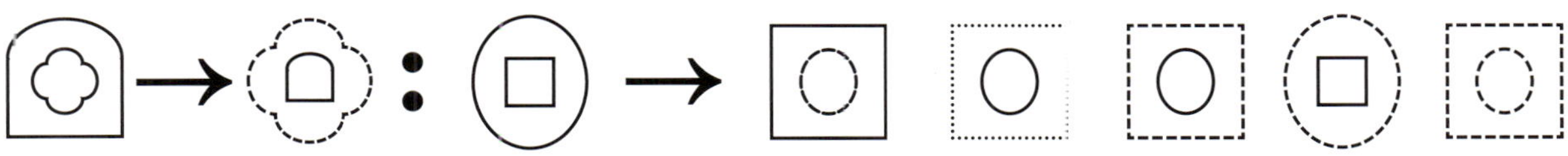

a b c d e

4)

a b c d e

5)

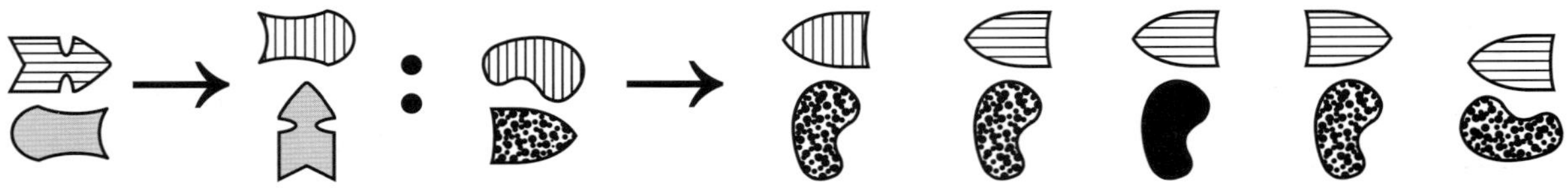

a b c d e

6)

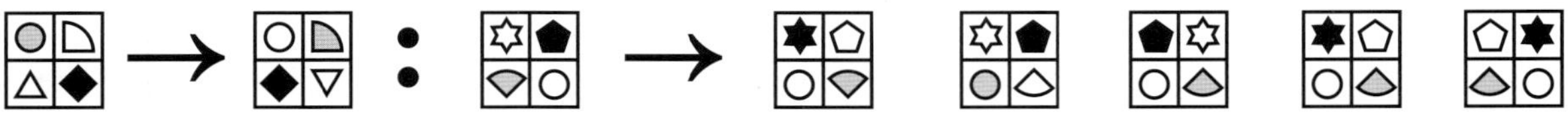

a b c d e

7)

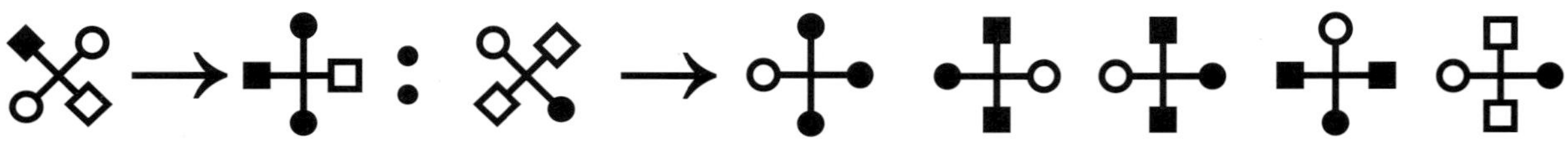

a b c d e

8)

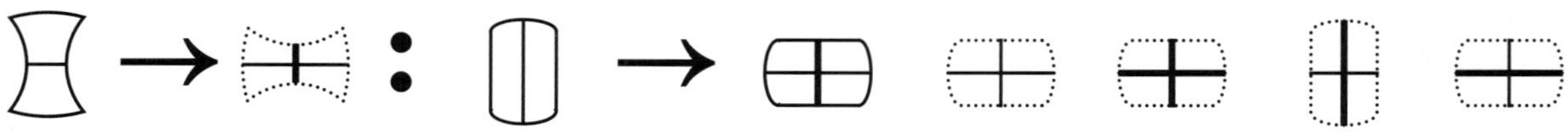

a b c d e

9)

a b c d e

Score

Section B

In the big square on the left of each line below, one of the small squares has been left empty. One of the five figures on the right should fill the empty square. Find this figure.

Example

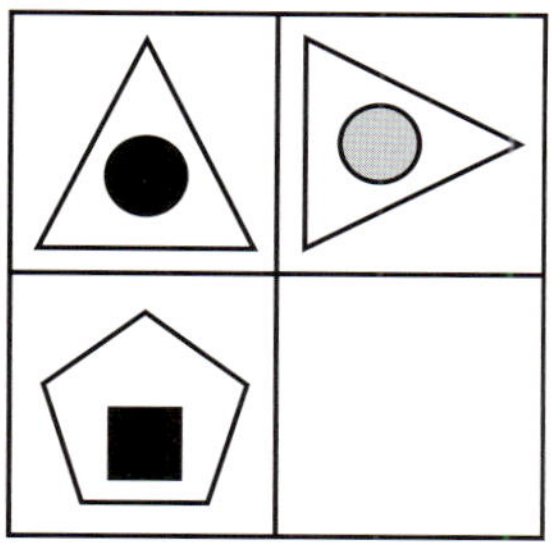

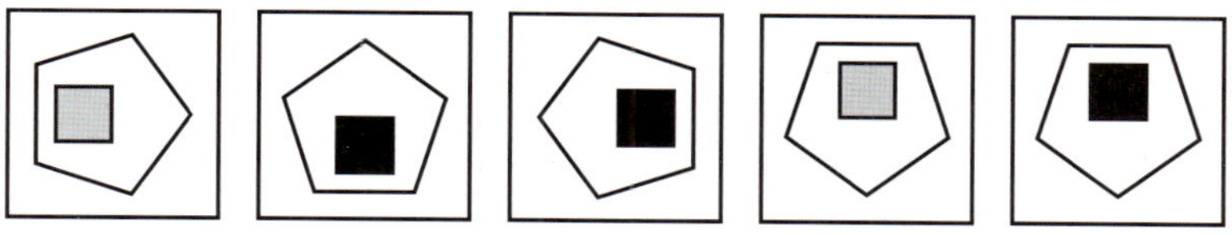

a b c d e

Now do the questions below. Circle the correct answer.

1)

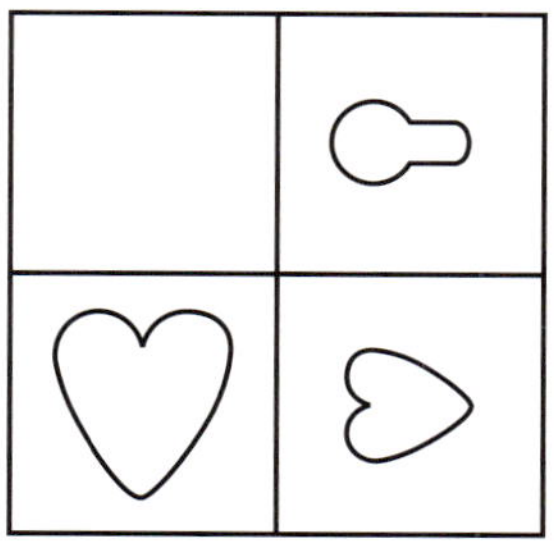

a b c d e

2)

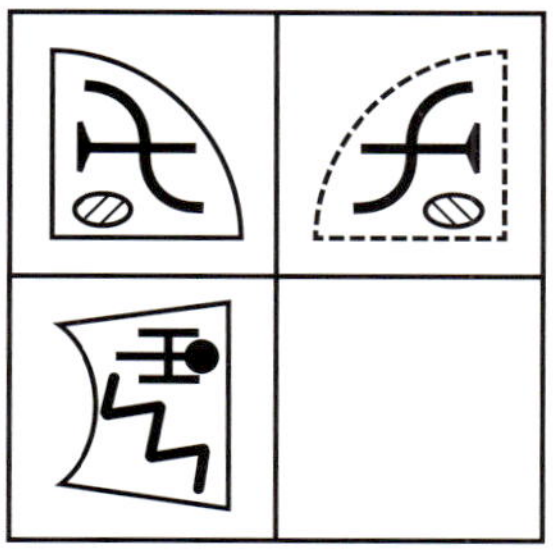

a b c d e

3)

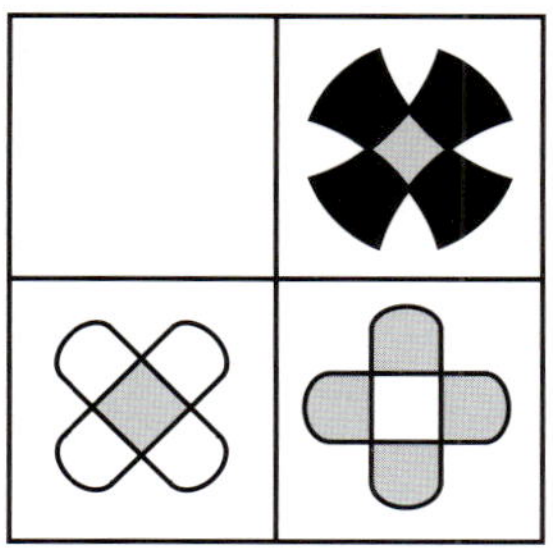

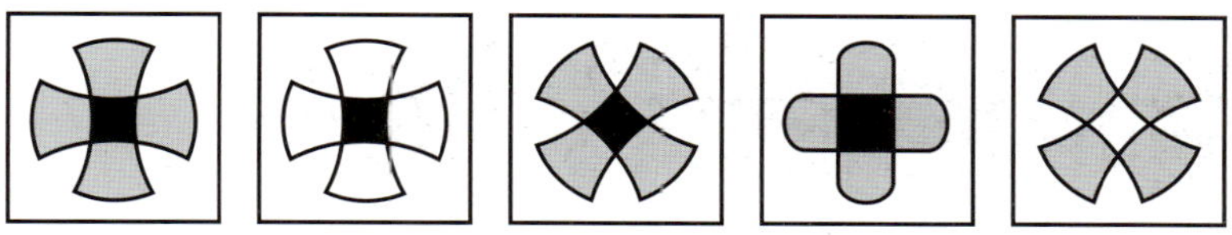

a b c d e

4)

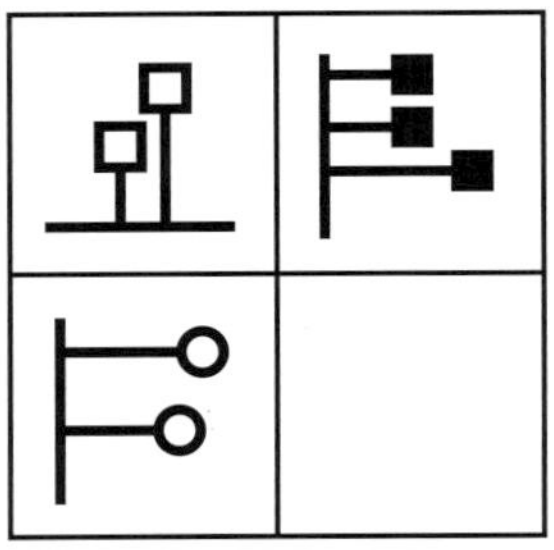

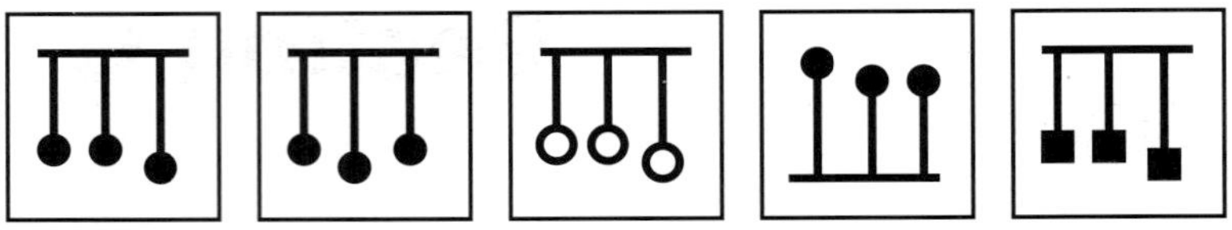

a b c d e

5)

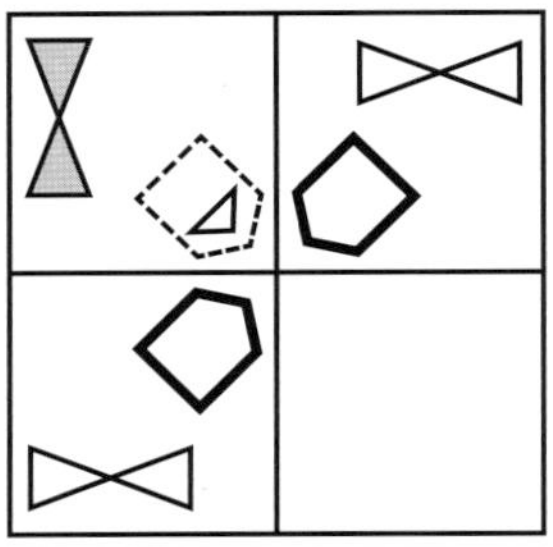

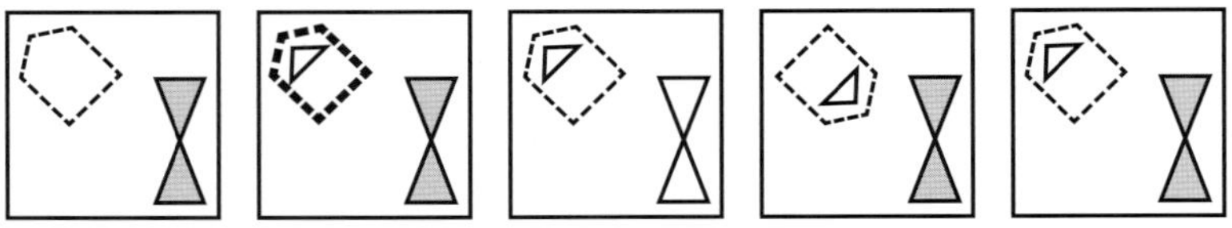

a b c d e

6)

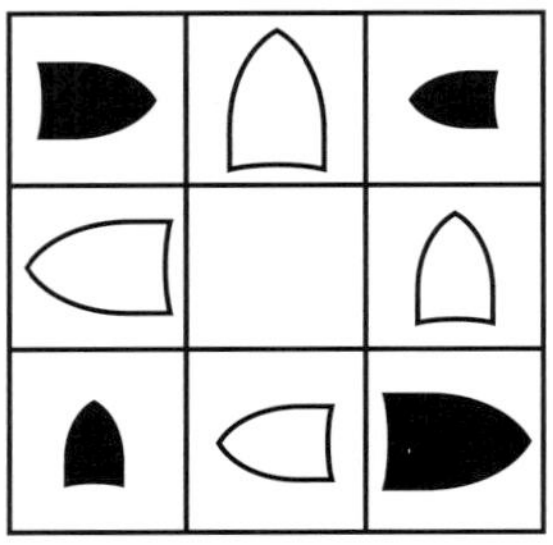

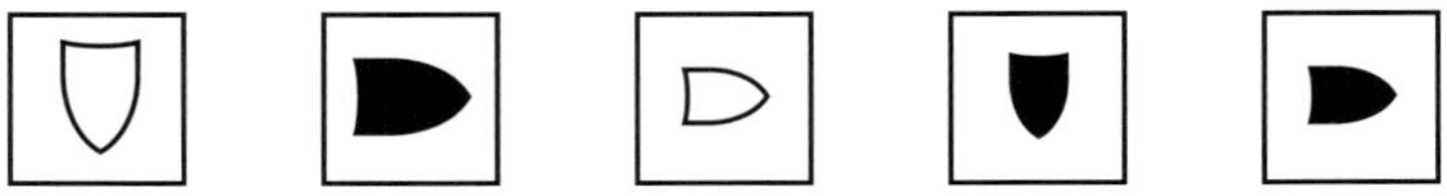

a b c d e

7)

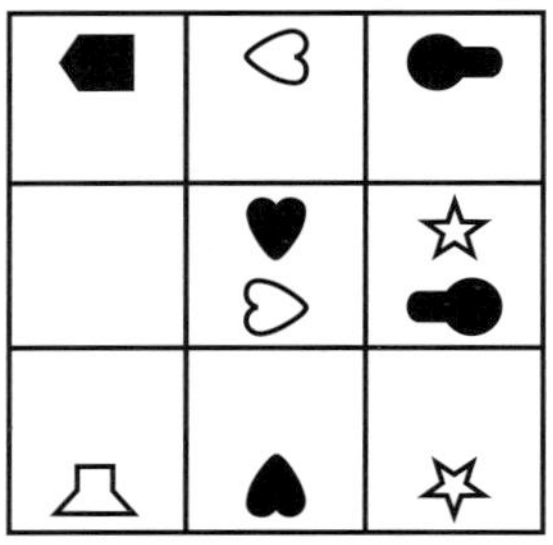

a b c d e

8)

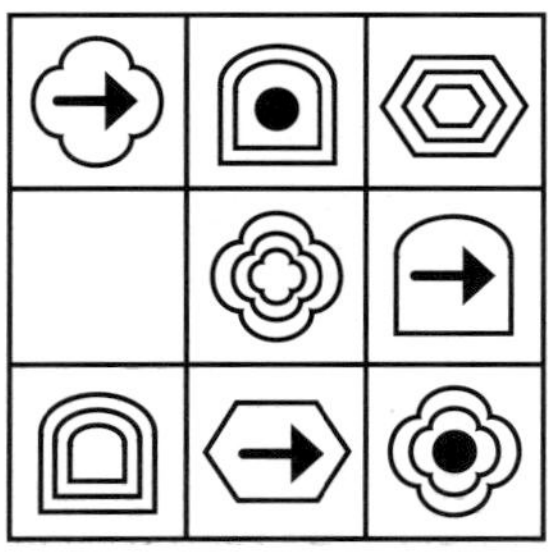

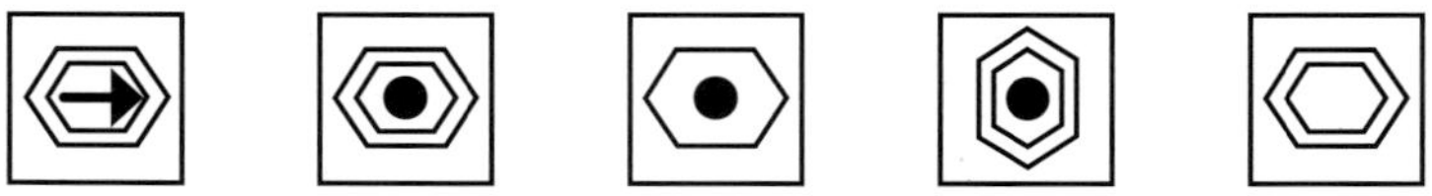

a b c d e

Score

Section C

The following figures correspond to the codes next to them. You must decide how the code letters go with the figures and then find the correct code for the Test Figure.

Example

 AZ

 BZ

 CY

TEST FIGURE

CZ	BY	AY	BZ	AZ
a	**b**	**(c)**	**d**	**e**

Now do the questions below. Circle the correct answer.

1)

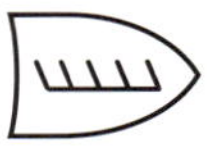 XL

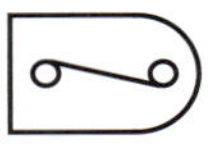 YM

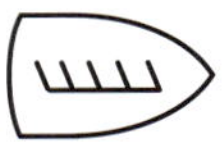 XN

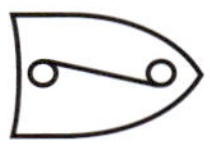

TEST FIGURE

XM	YN	XL	YL	YM
a	**b**	**c**	**d**	**e**

2)

 JAG

 JBH

 KAI

TEST FIGURE

KBG	KAG	JBG	KBH	KBI
a	**b**	**c**	**d**	**e**

3)

 WDM

 XEN

 WEO

 XFN

TEST FIGURE

WDO	XFO	WFO	XEO	XFN
a	**b**	**c**	**d**	**e**

4)  AEP

 BFQ

 BER

TEST FIGURE

AER	BEQ	AFQ	AEQ	AFR
a	**b**	**c**	**d**	**e**

5)  SZF

 SYG

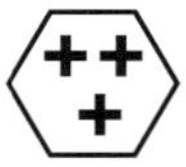 TXF

TEST FIGURE

SZG	TYG	SXF	TZG	TXG
a	**b**	**c**	**d**	**e**

6)  LDU

 MEV

 MFW

 NDV

TEST FIGURE

MFU	LEU	LFU	LFV	NFU
a	**b**	**c**	**d**	**e**

7)  JWA

 KXB

 JYB

 LZC

TEST FIGURE

LWA	LXA	JXA	LYA	KZB
a	**b**	**c**	**d**	**e**

8)  RCLX

 SDMY

 TEMX

 TDLZ

TEST FIGURE

SCMZ	SCMX	RCMY	TCLZ	SDMZ
a	**b**	**c**	**d**	**e**

Score

Section D

On the left of each of the rows below there are two figures that are alike. On the right there are five more figures. Find which one of these five is **most like** the two figures on the left.

Example

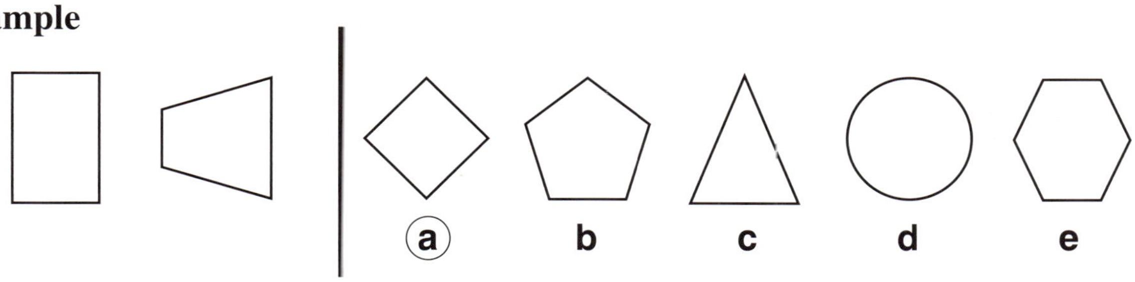

Now do the questions below. Circle the correct answer.

1)

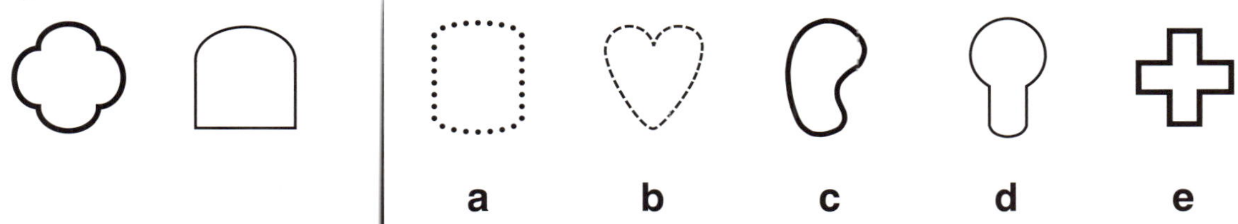

2)

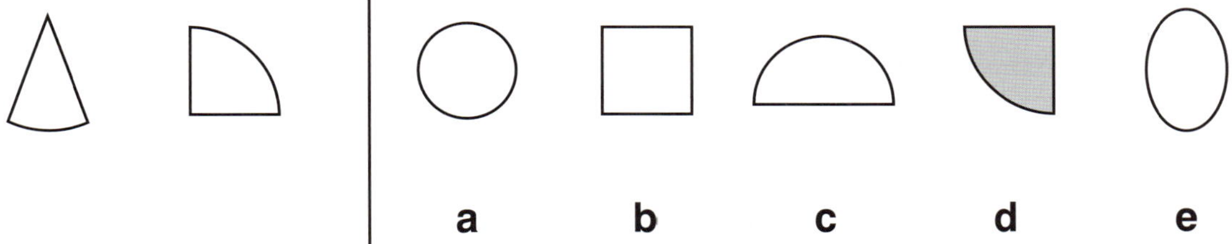

3)

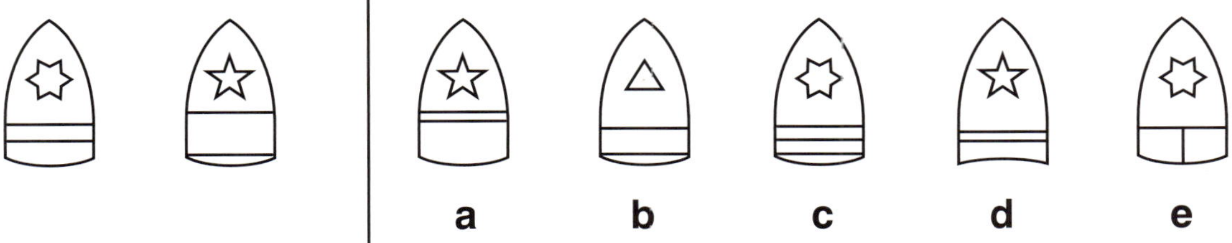

4)

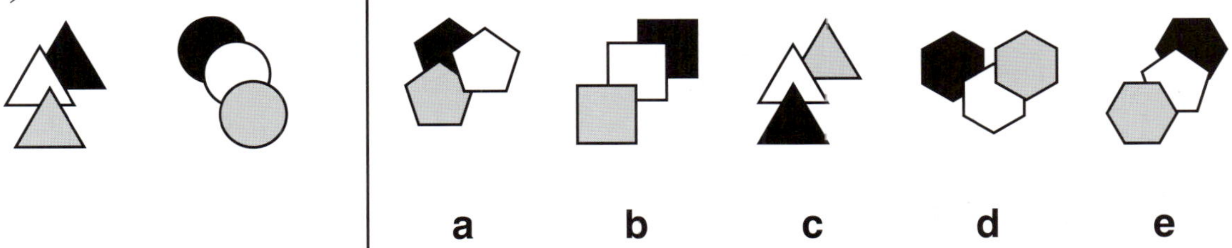

5)

a b c d e

6)

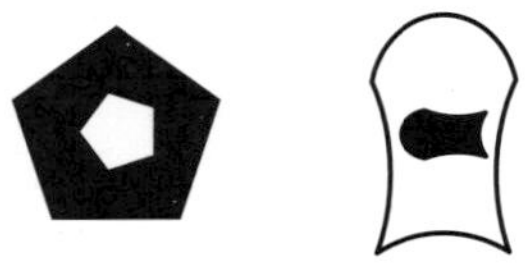

a b c d e

7)

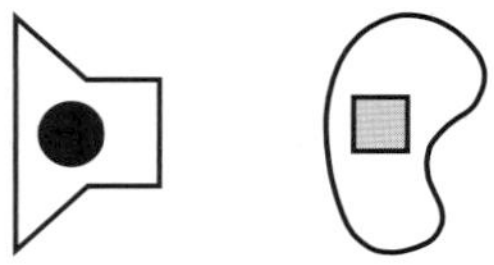

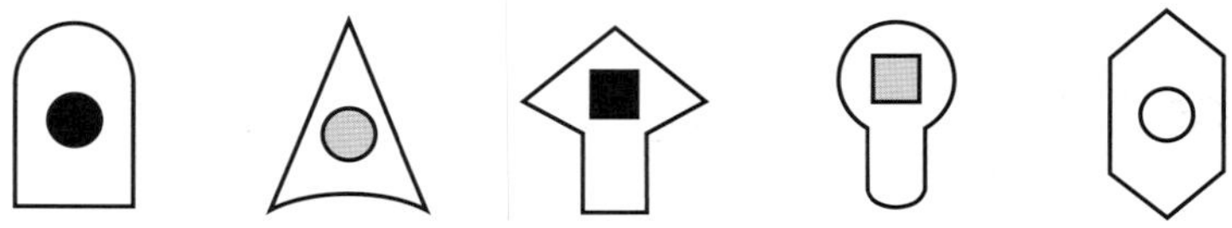

a b c d e

8)

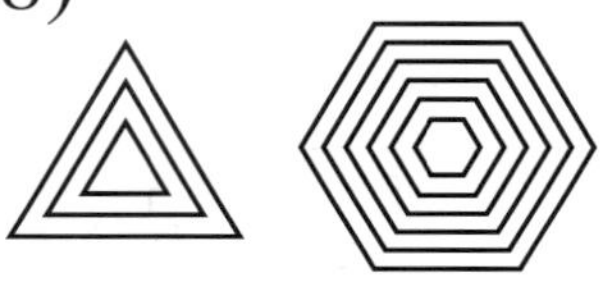

a b c d e

9)

a b c d e

10)

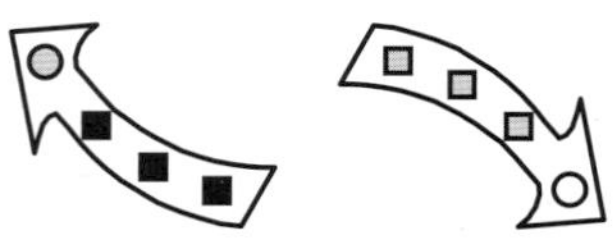

a b c d e

Score

Non-verbal Reasoning Test 5

Section A

To the left of each of the lines below there are five squares arranged in order. One of these squares has been left empty. Find which one of the five squares on the right should take the place of the empty square.

Example

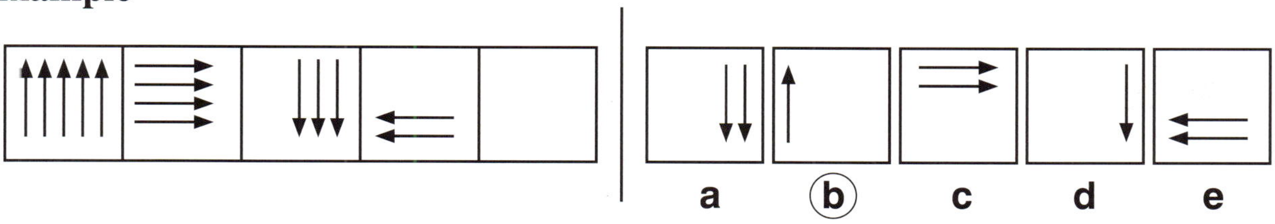

Now do the questions below. Circle the correct answer.

1)

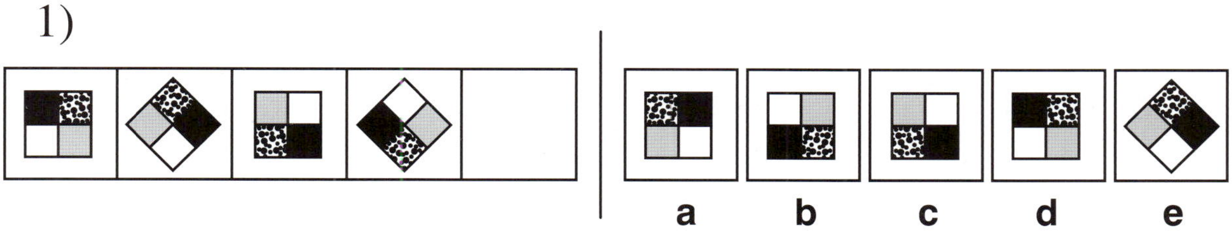

2)

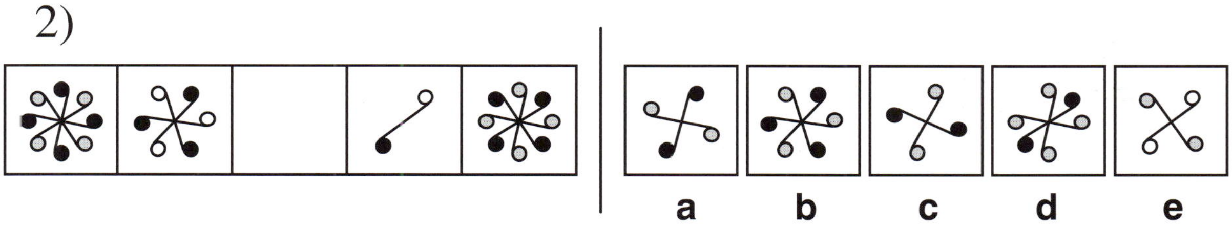

3)

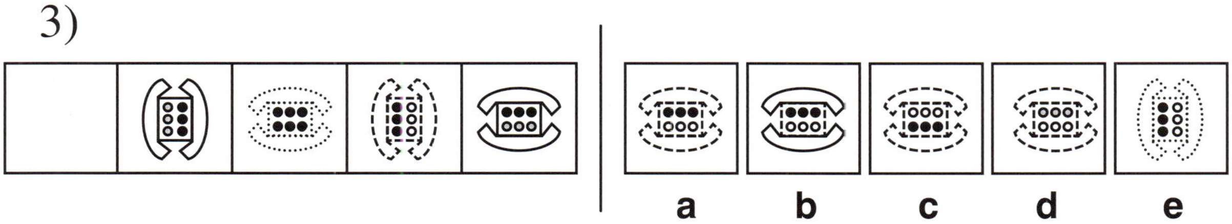

4)

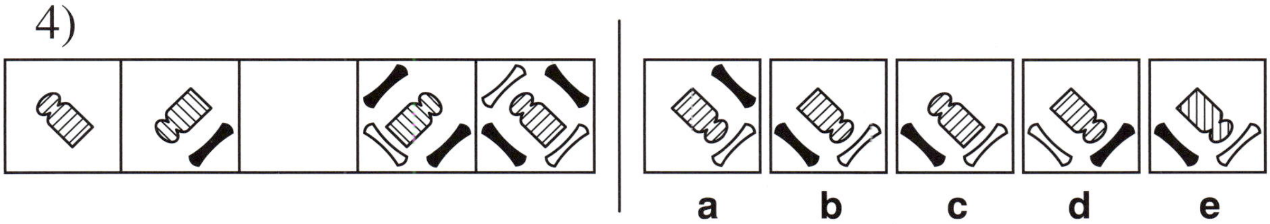

5)

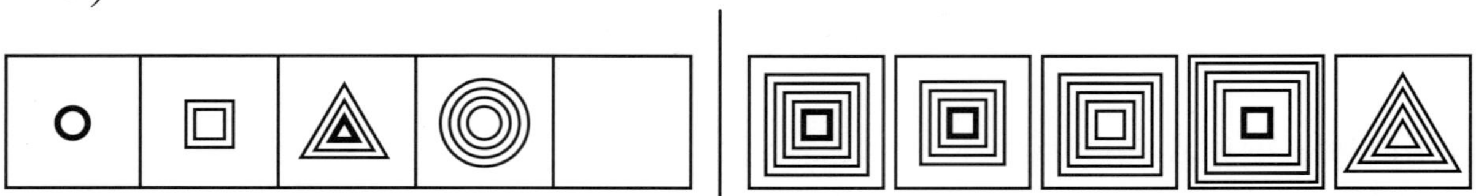

a b c d e

6)

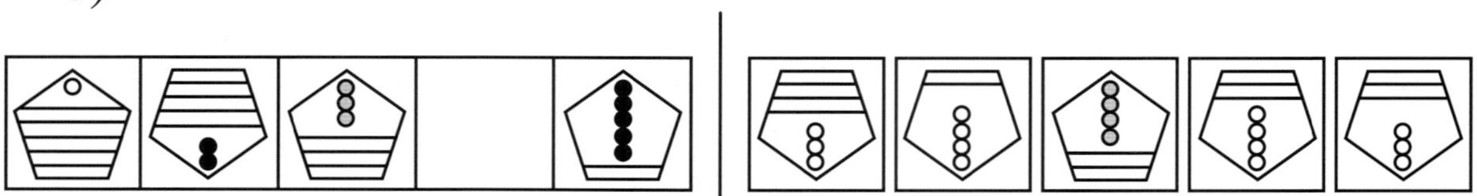

a b c d e

7)

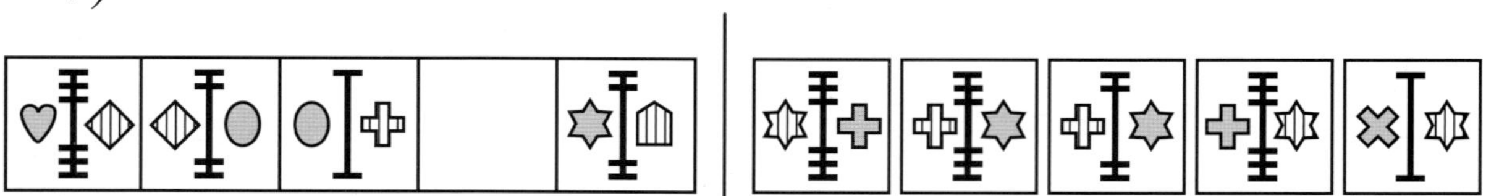

a b c d e

8)

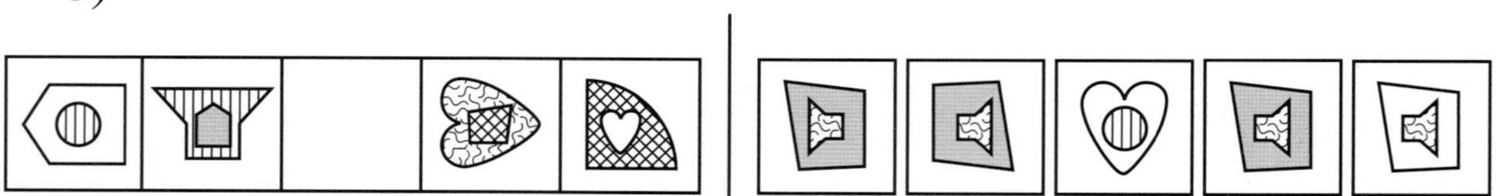

a b c d e

9)

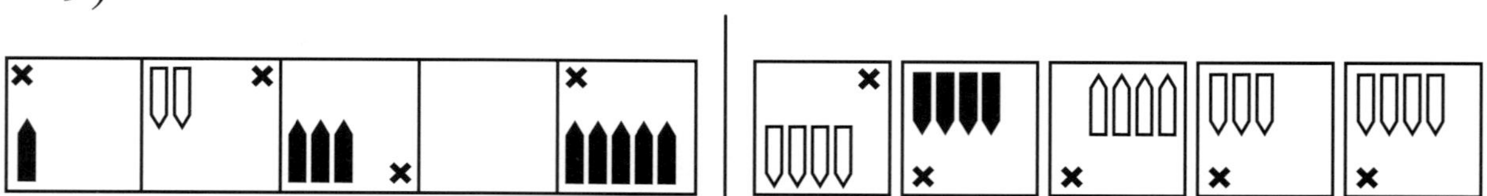

a b c d e

Score

Section B

On the left of each row are two figures with an arrow between them. Decide how the second figure is related to the first. After these there is a third figure, then an arrow and then five more figures. Decide which of the five figures goes with the third figure to make a pair like the two figures on the left.

Example

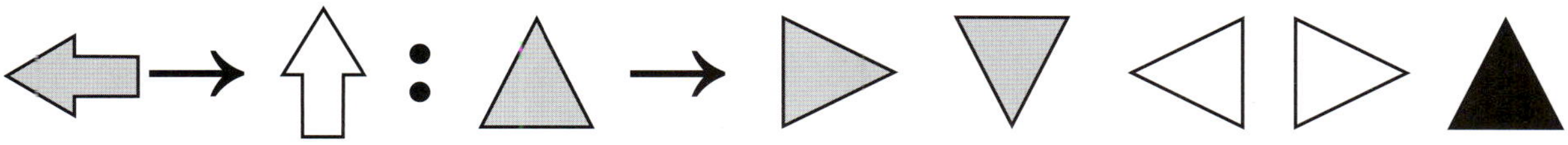

a b c ⓓ e

Now do the questions below. Circle the correct answer.

1)

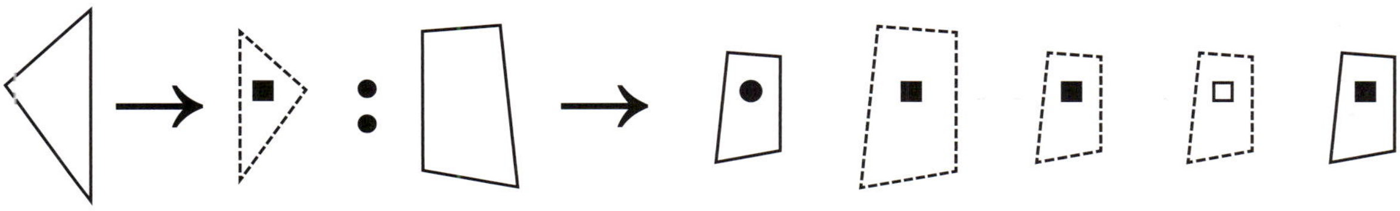

a b c d e

2)

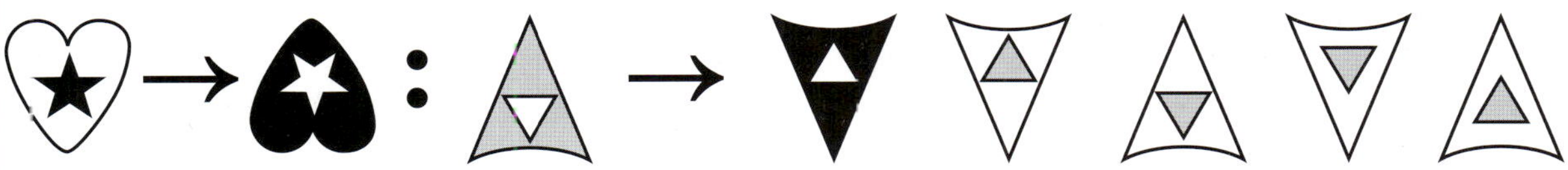

a b c d e

3)

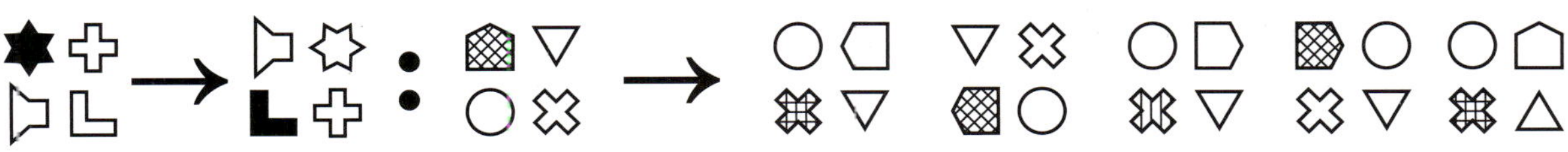

a b c d e

4)

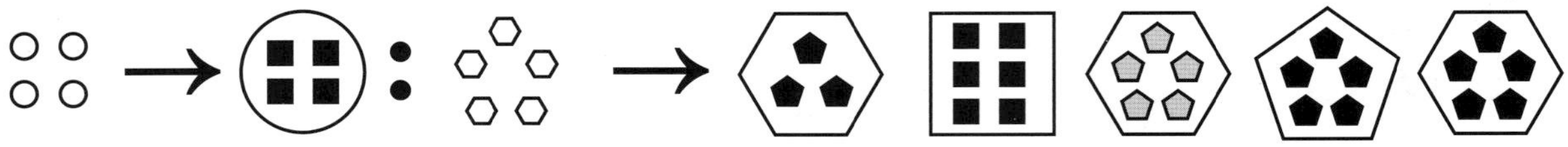

a b c d e

5)

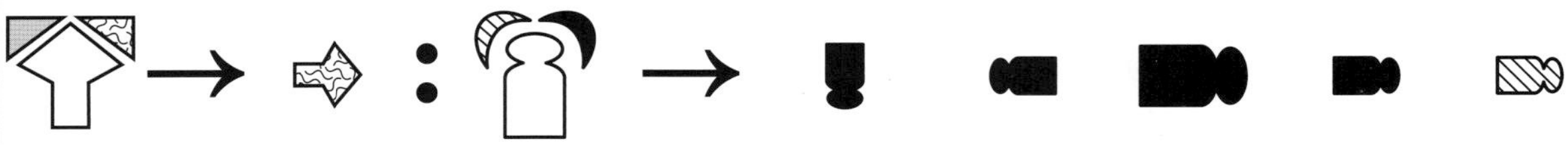

a b c d e

6)

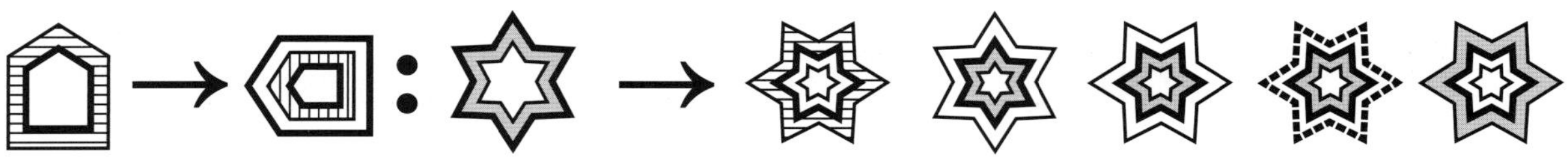

a b c d e

7)

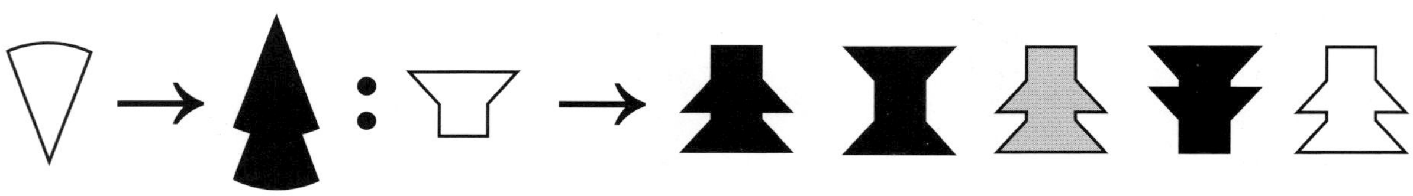

a b c d e

8)

a b c d e

Score

Section C

In each of the rows below there are five figures. Find one figure in each row that is **most unlike** the other four.

Example

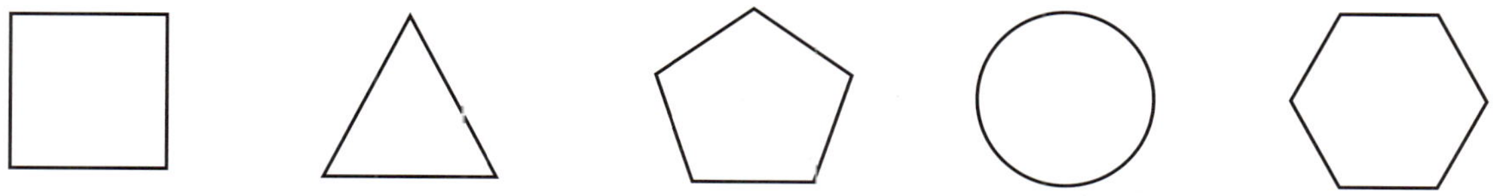

a b c (d) e

Now do the questions below. Circle the correct answer.

1)

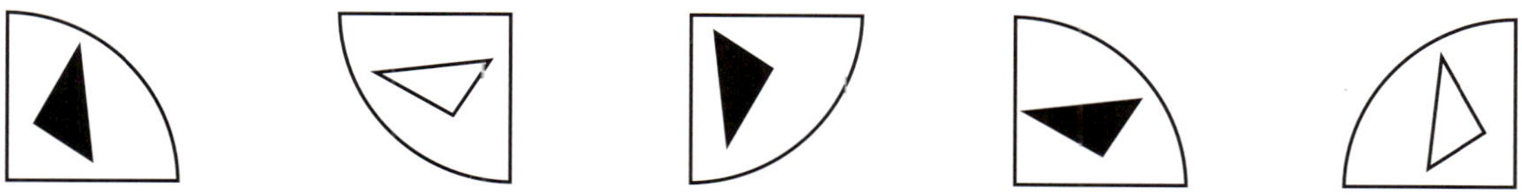

a b c d e

2)

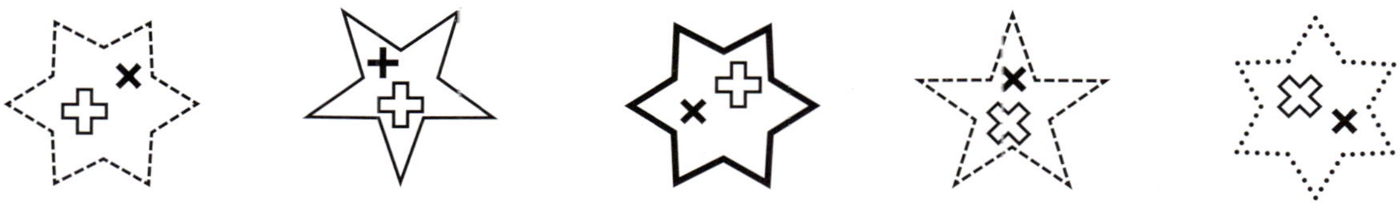

a b c d e

3)

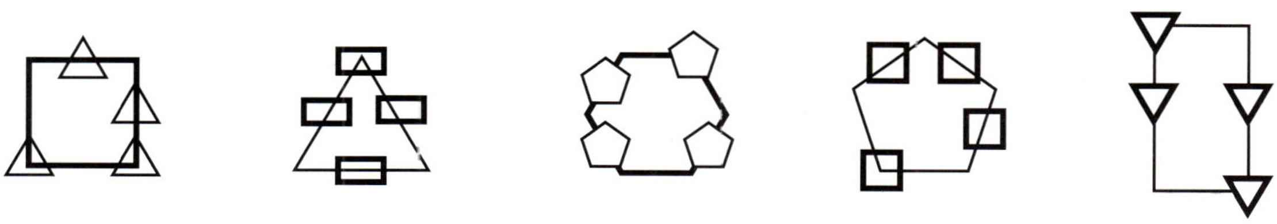

a b c d e

4)

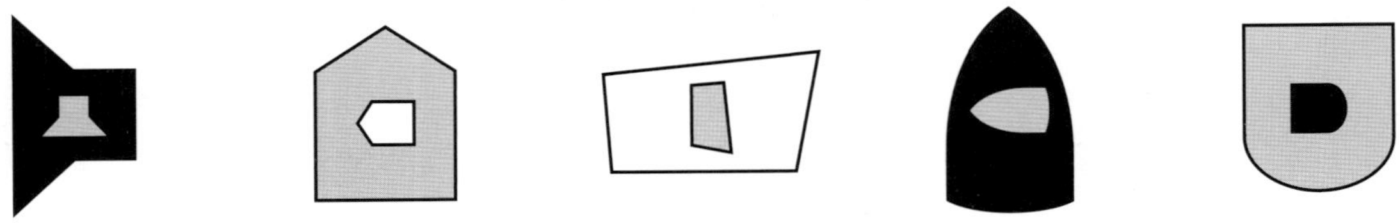

a b c d e

5)

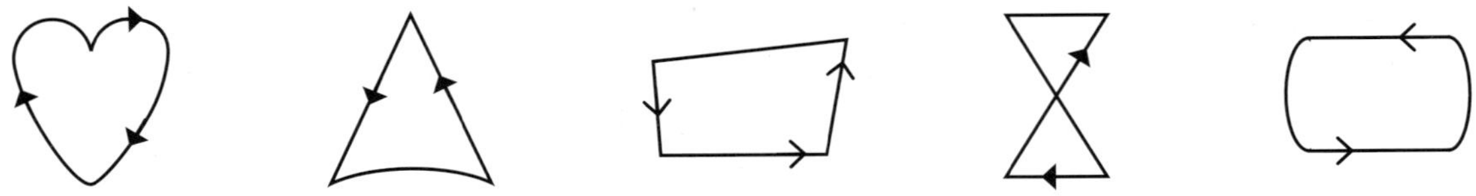

a b c d e

6)

a b c d e

7)

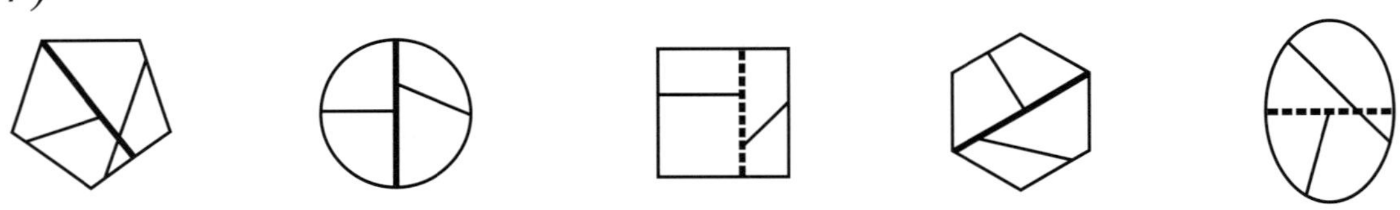

a b c d e

8)

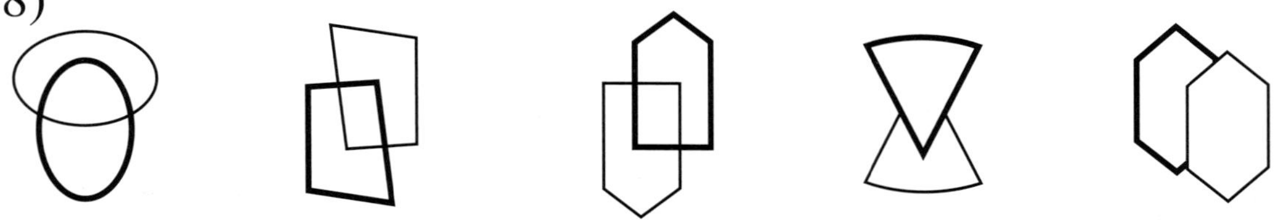

a b c d e

Score

Section D

The following figures correspond to the codes next to them. You must decide how the code letters go with the figures and then find the correct code for the Test Figure.

Example

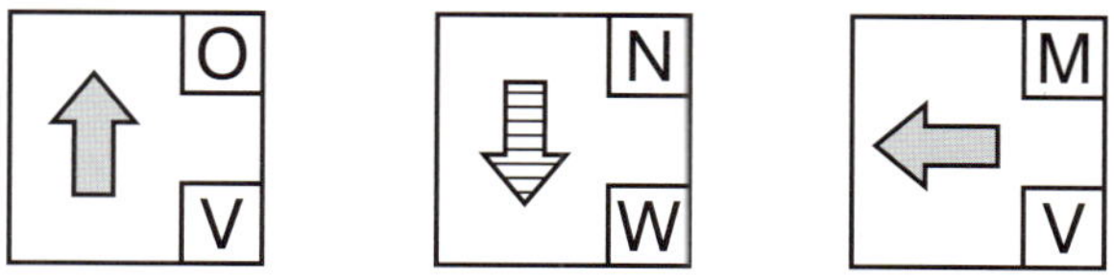

TEST FIGURE

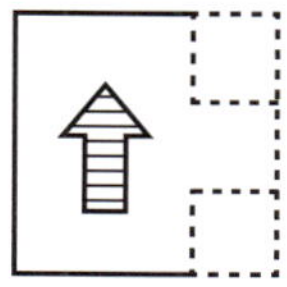

a	b	c	d	e
O V	N V	M W	(O W)	M V

Now do the questions below. Circle the correct answer.

1)

TEST FIGURE

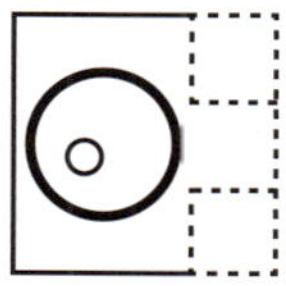

a	b	c	d	e
S A	R A	T B	R B	T A

2)

TEST FIGURE

a	b	c	d	e
H M	G N	G O	H N	H O

3)

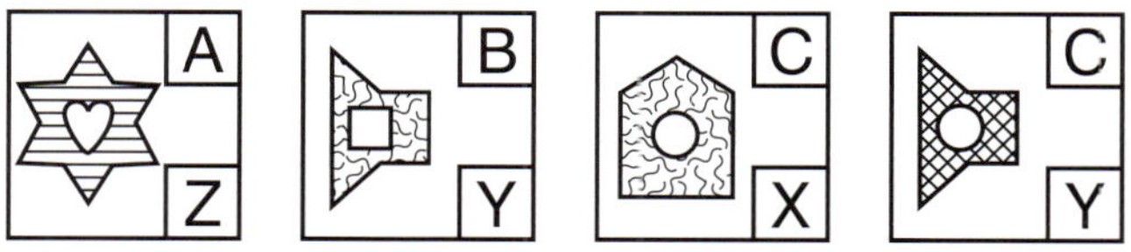

TEST FIGURE

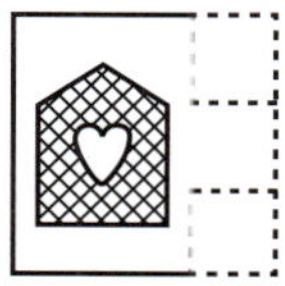

a	b	c	d	e
A Y	B X	B Z	C Z	A X

4)

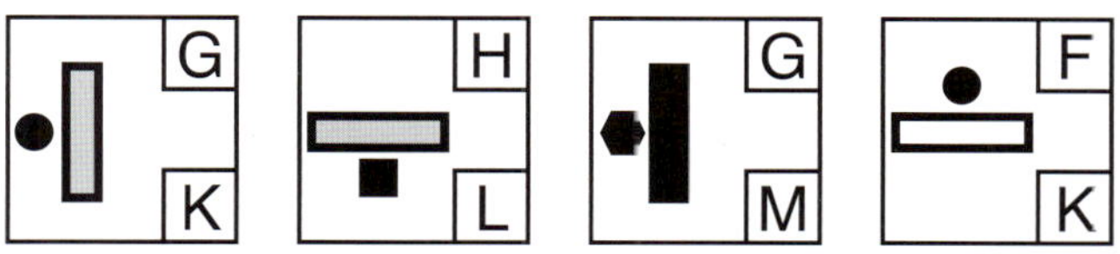

TEST FIGURE

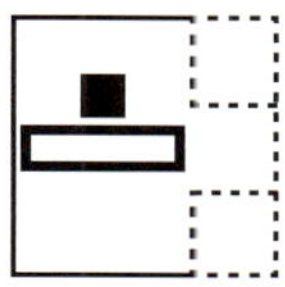

a	b	c	d	e
F M	G L	H K	F L	H M

5)

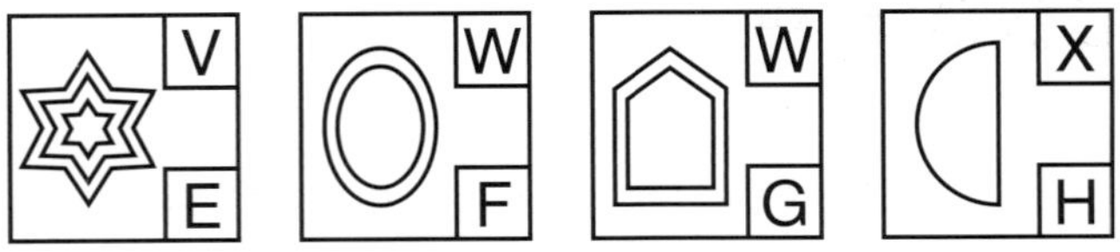

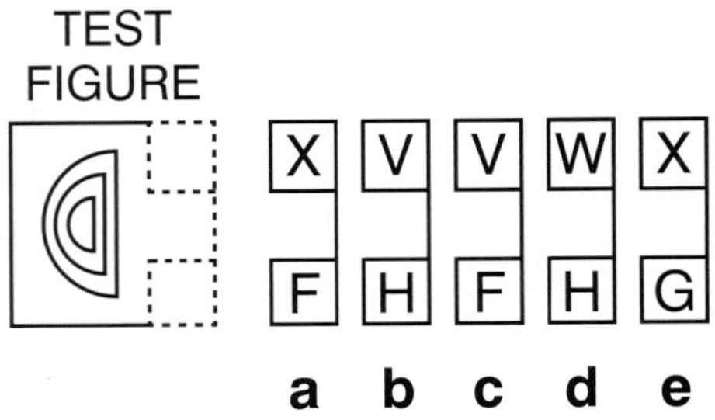

6)

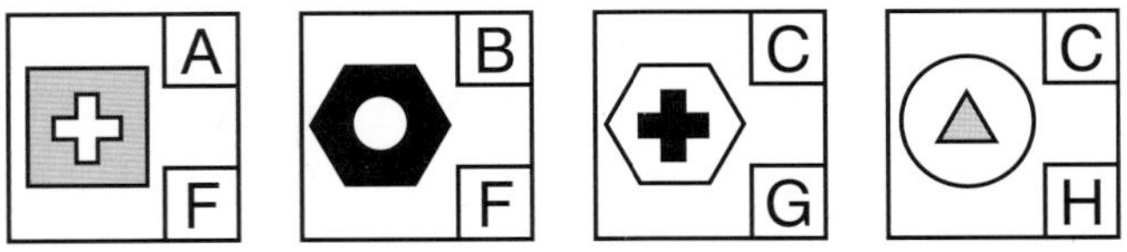

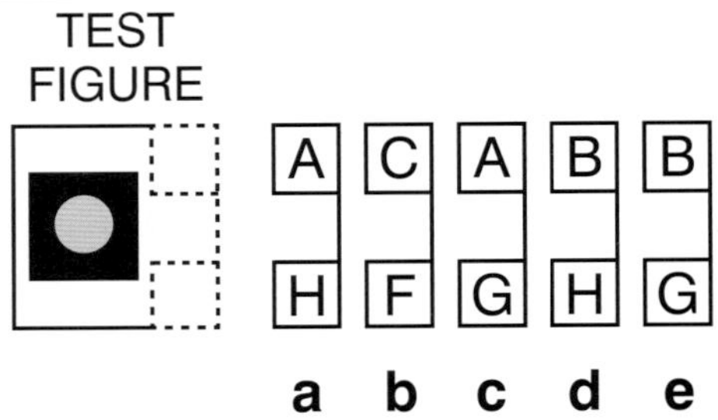

7)

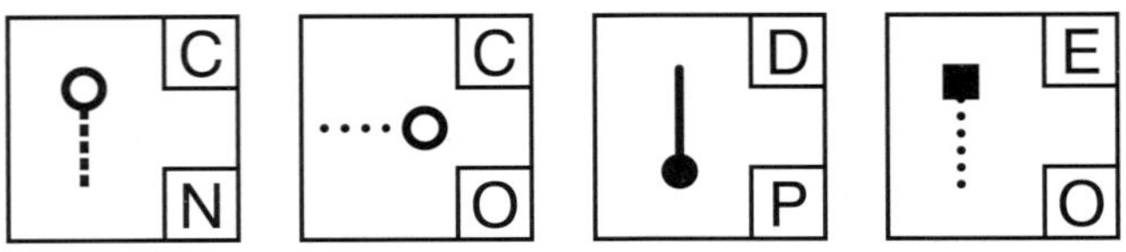

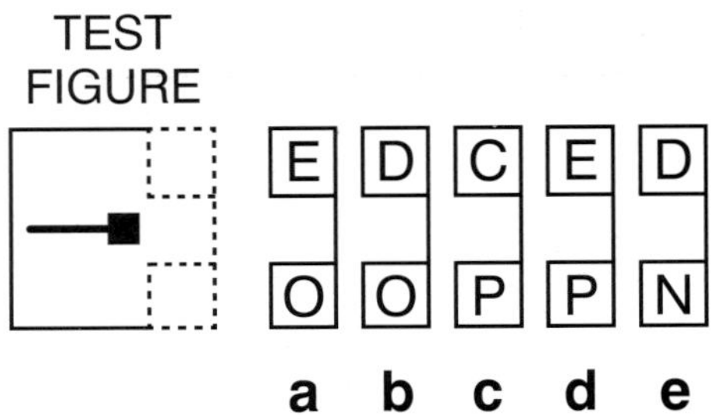

8)

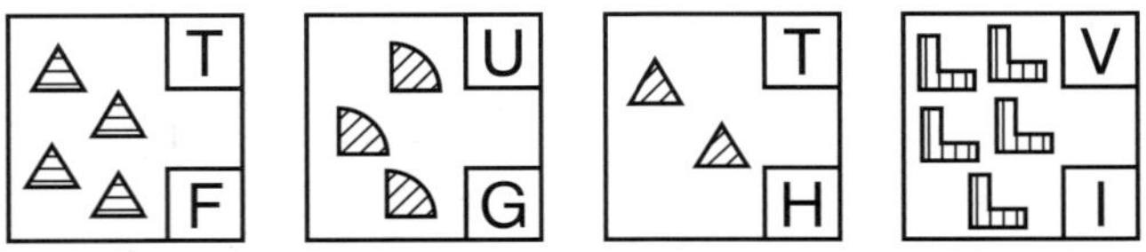

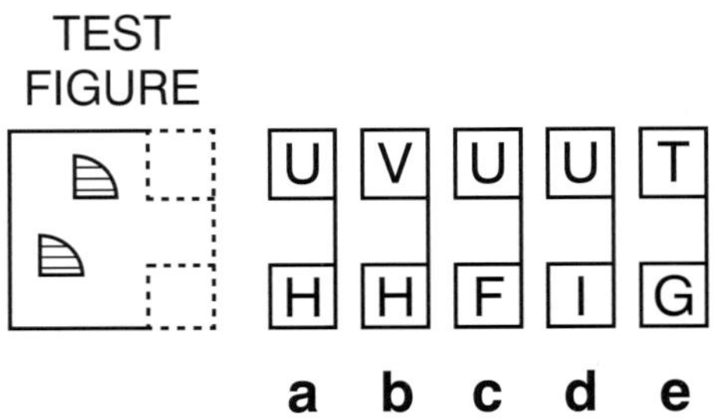

9)

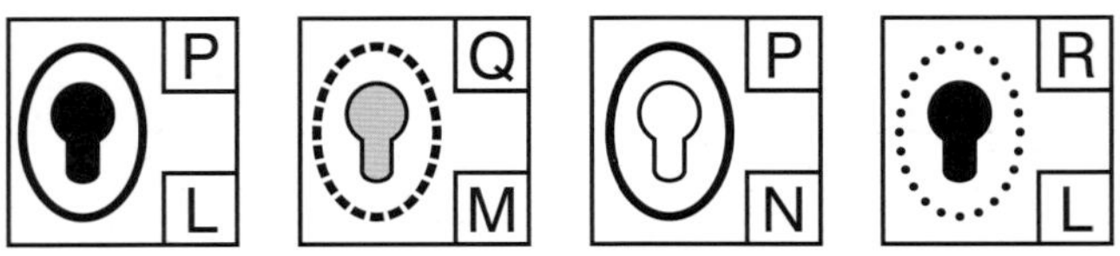

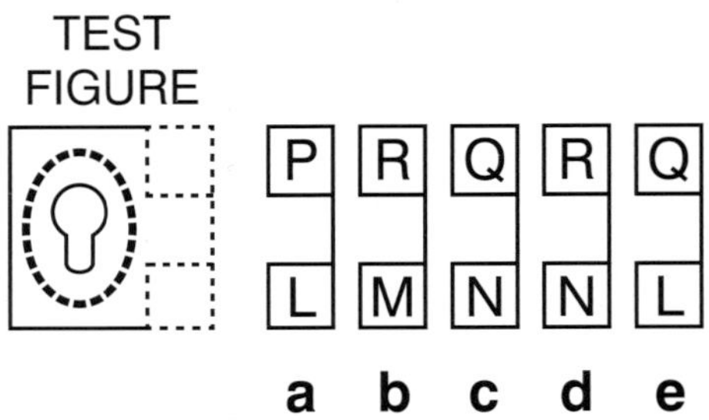

10)

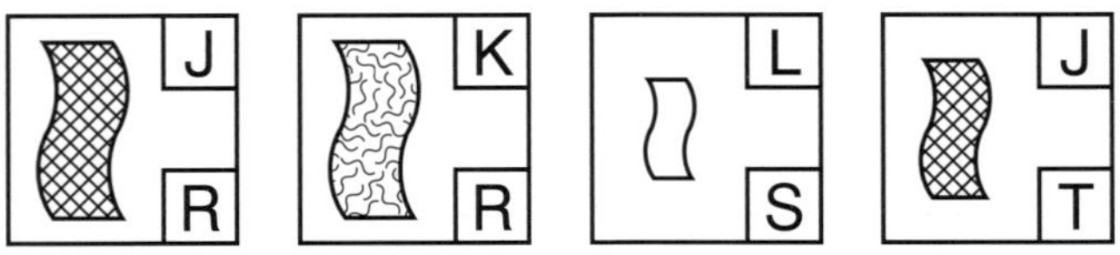

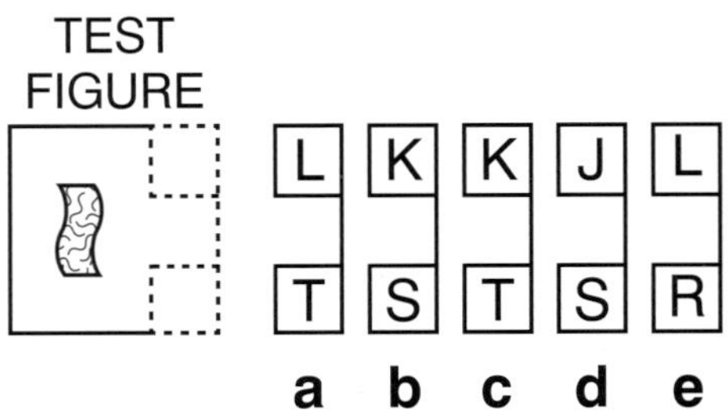

Score

Non-verbal Reasoning Test 6

Section A

On the left of each of the rows below there are two figures that are alike. On the right there are five more figures. Find which one of these five is **most like** the two figures on the left.

Example

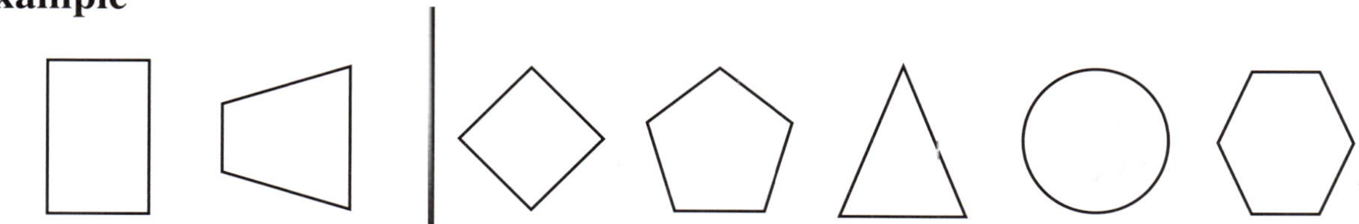

(a) b c d e

Now do the questions below. Circle the correct answer.

1)

a b c d e

2)

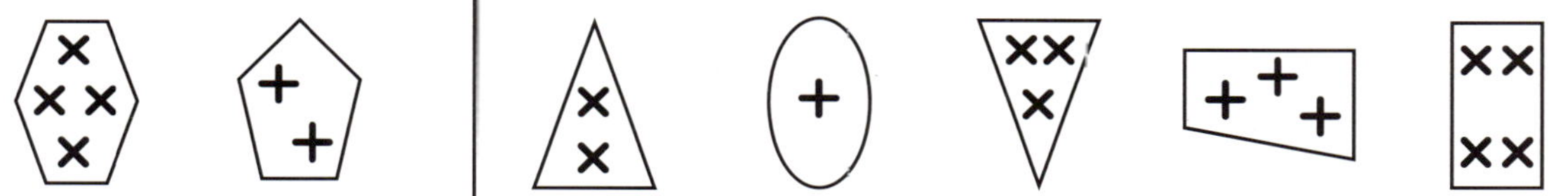

a b c d e

3)

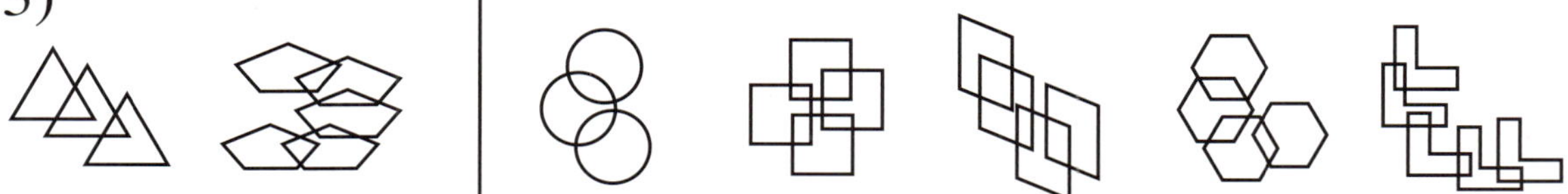

a b c d e

4)

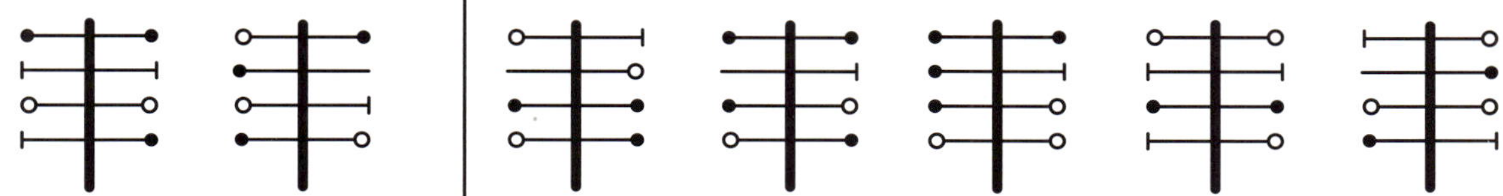

a b c d e

5)

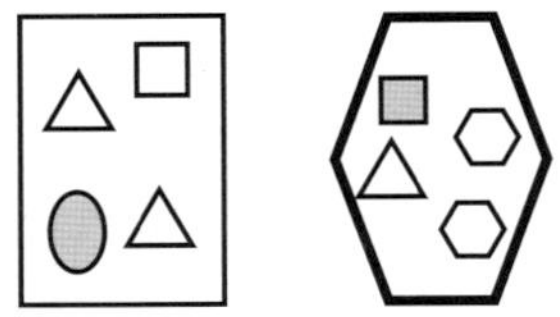

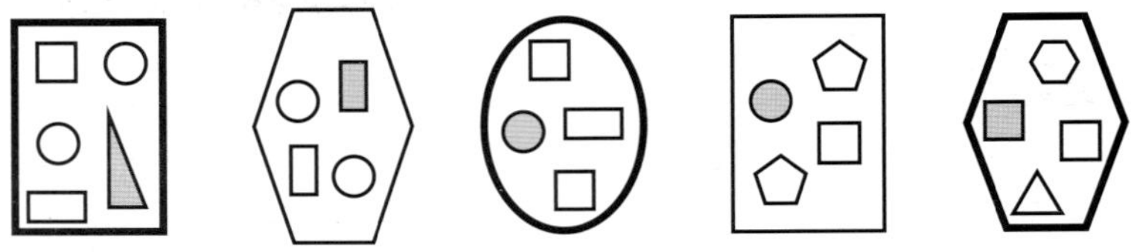

a b c d e

6)

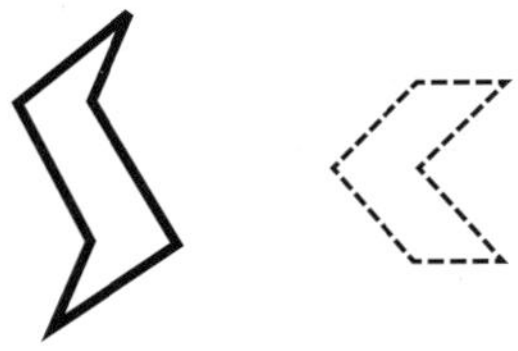

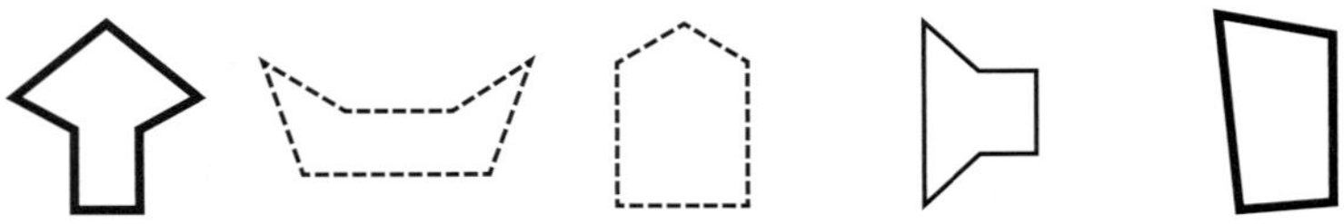

a b c d e

7)

a b c d e

8)

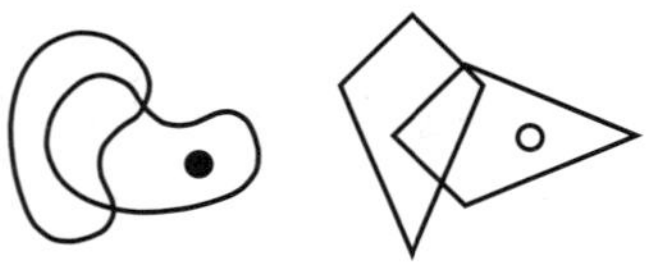

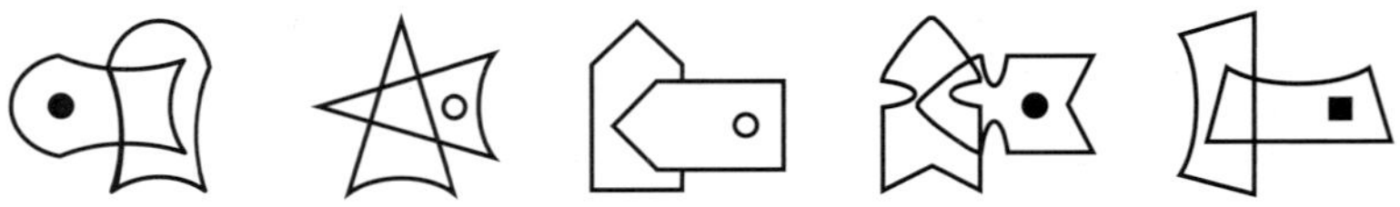

a b c d e

9)

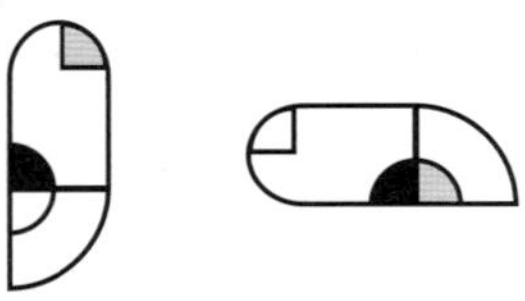

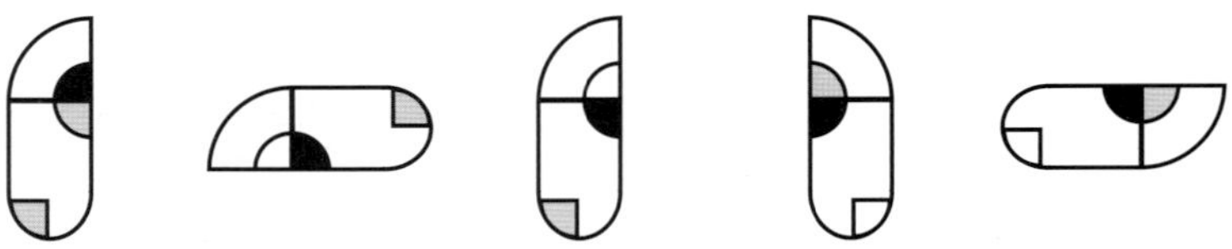

a b c d e

Score

Section B

In the big square on the left of each line below, one of the small squares has been left empty. One of the five figures on the right should fill the empty square. Find this figure.

Example

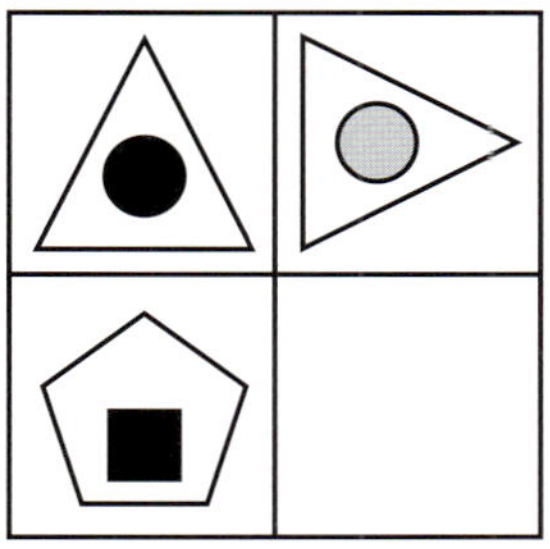

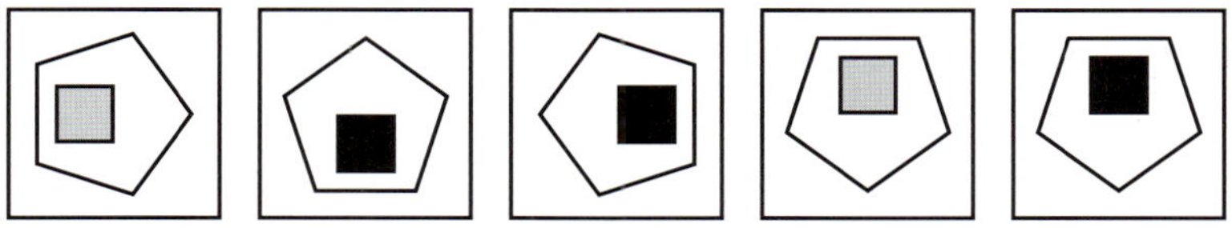

(a) b c d e

Now do the questions below. Circle the correct answer.

1)

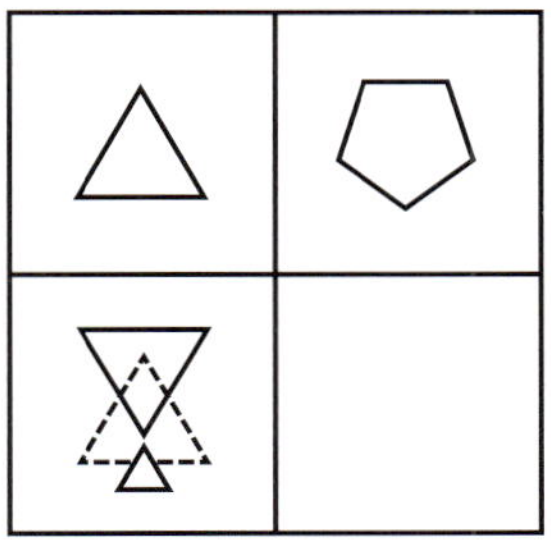

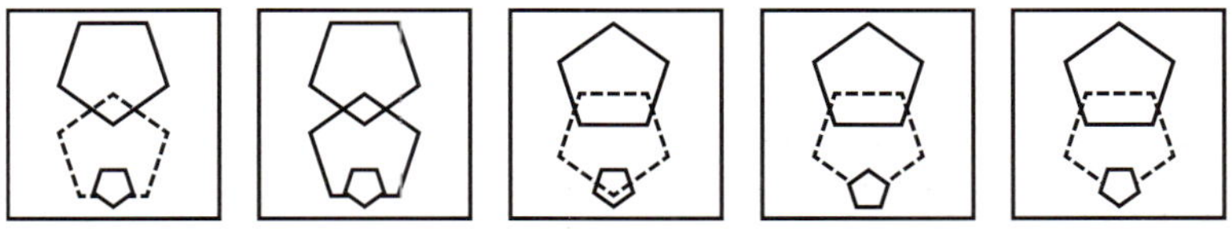

a b c d e

2)

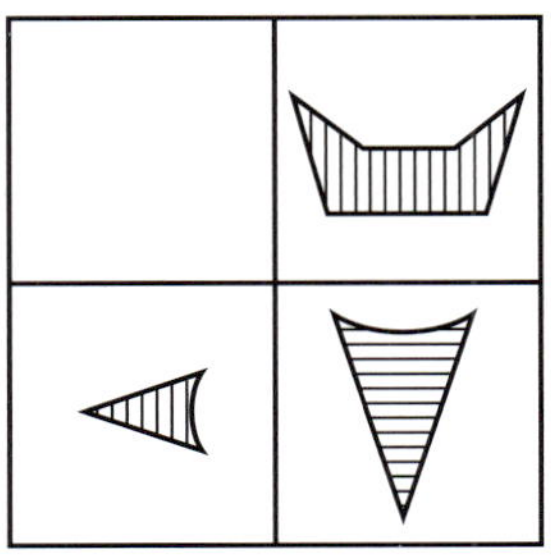

a b c d e

3)

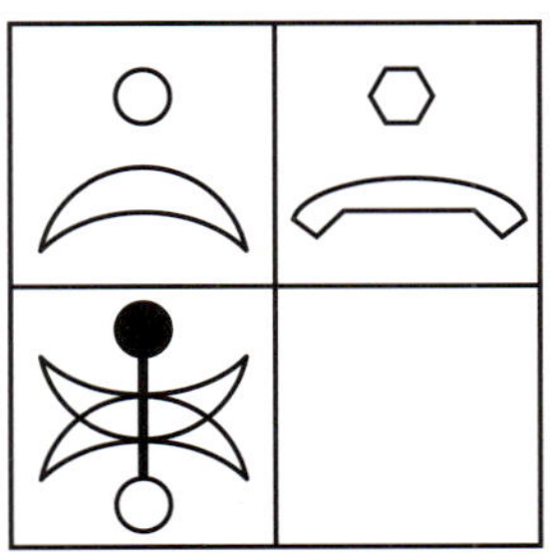

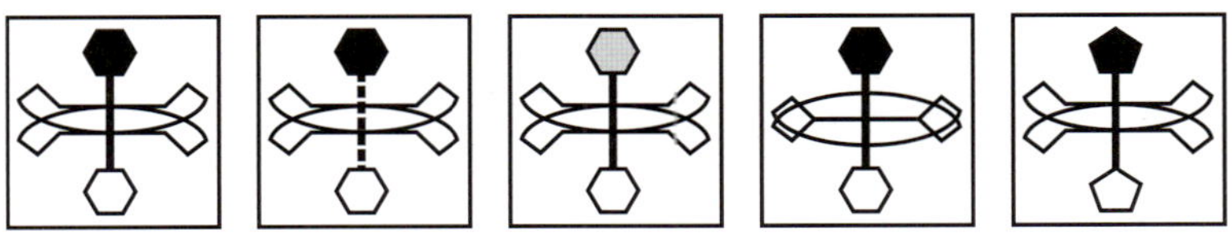

a b c d e

4)

a b c d e

5)

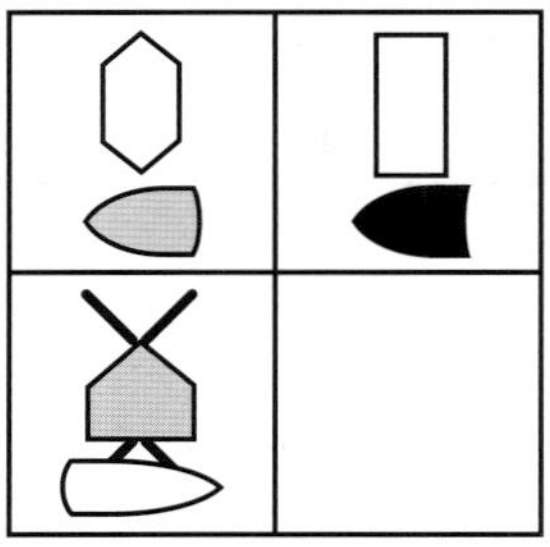

a b c d e

6)

a b c d e

7)

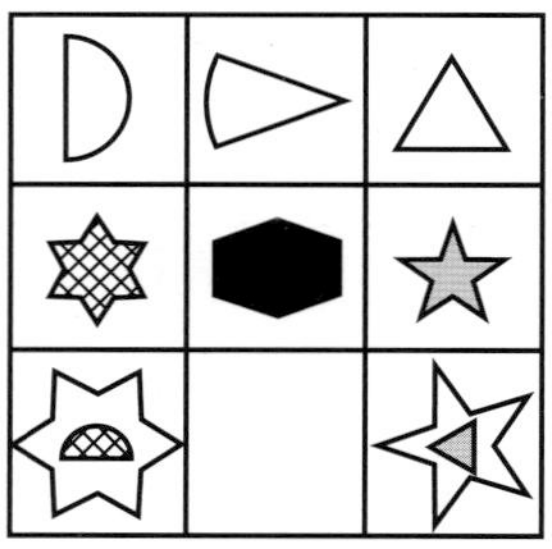

a b c d e

8)

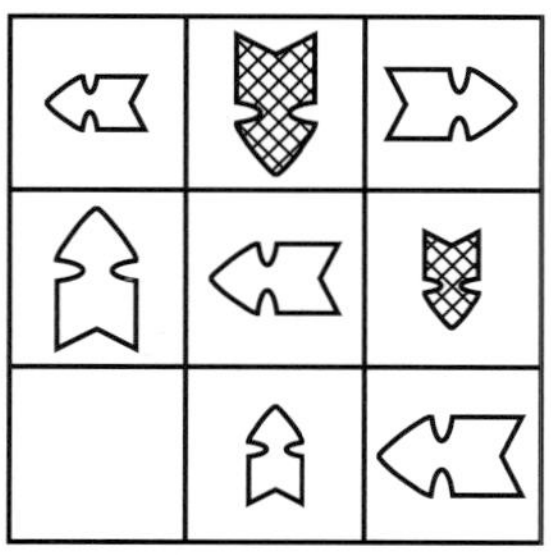

a b c d e

Score

Section C

To the left of each of the lines below there are five squares arranged in order. One of these squares has been left empty. Find which one of the five squares on the right should take the place of the empty square.

Example

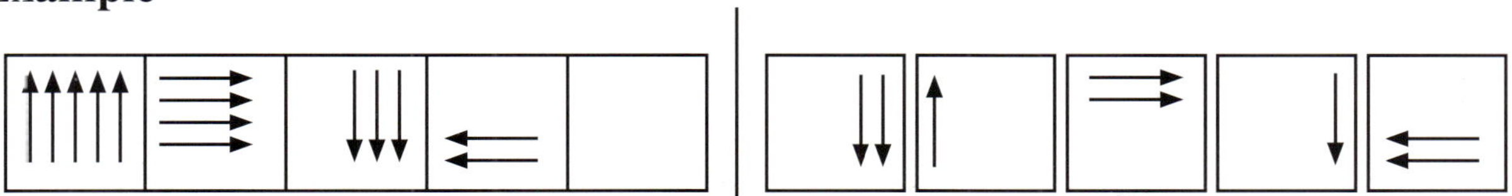

a (b) c d e

Now do the questions below. Circle the correct answer.

1)

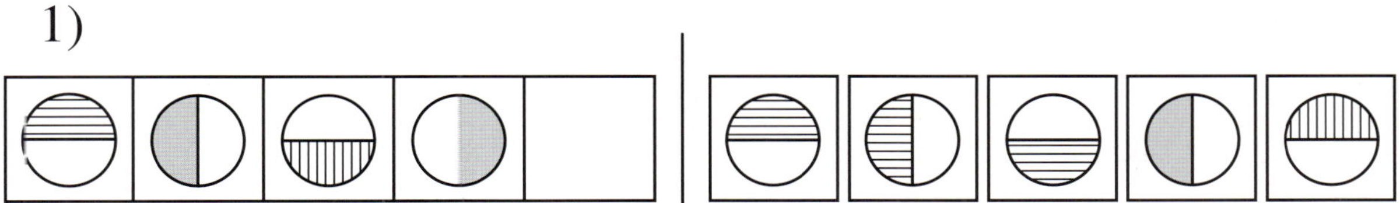

a b c d e

2)

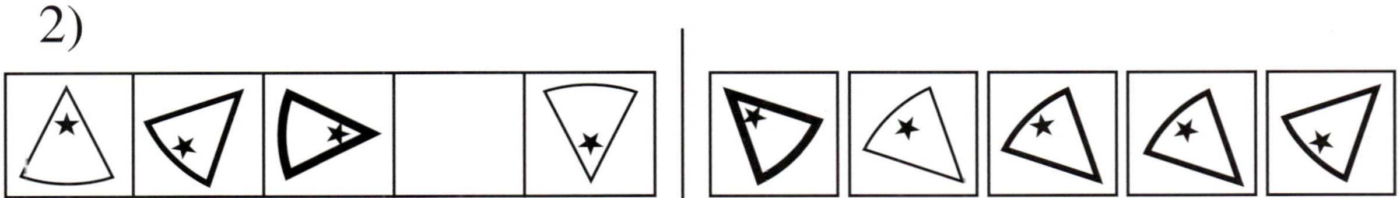

a b c d e

3)

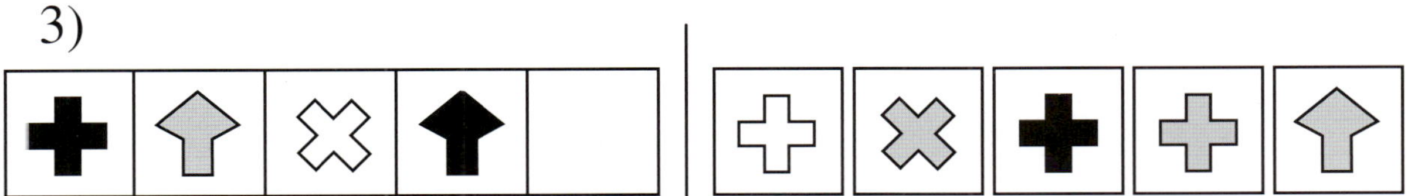

a b c d e

4)

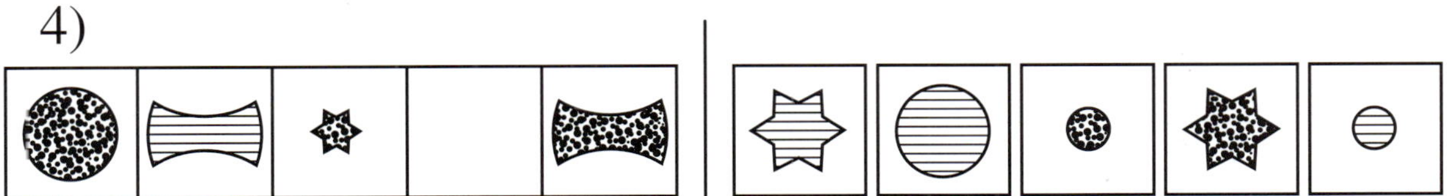

a b c d e

5)

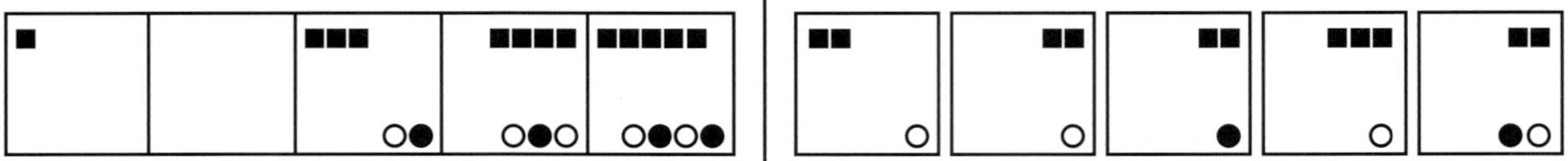

a b c d e

6)

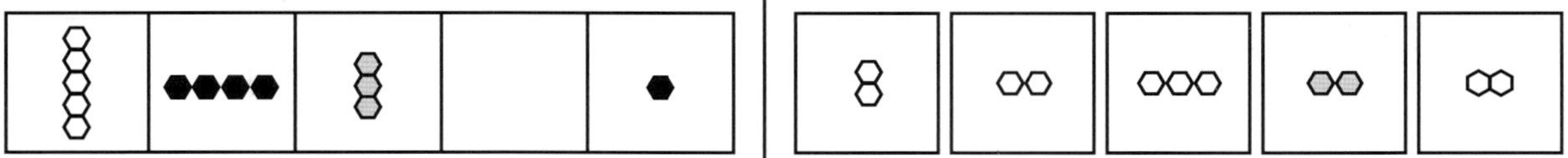

a b c d e

7)

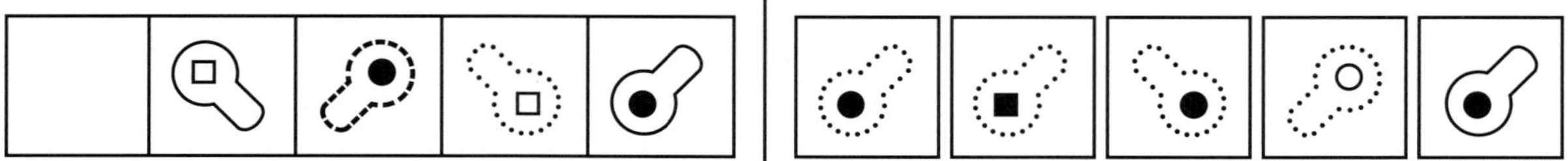

a b c d e

8)

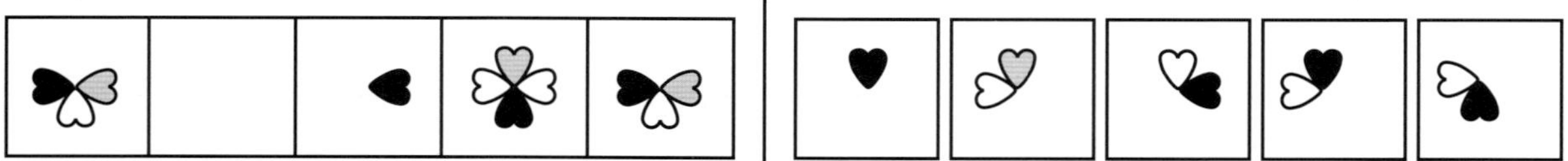

a b c d e

9)

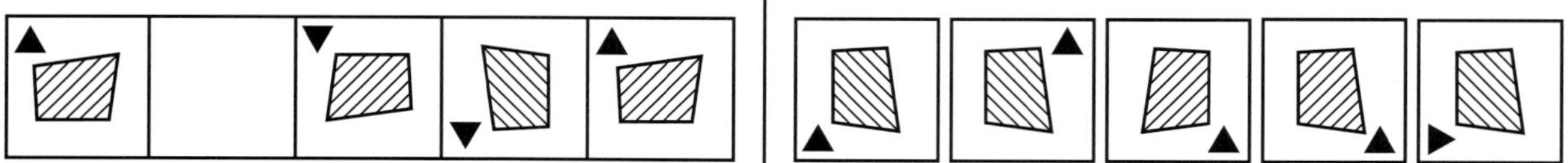

a b c d e

10)

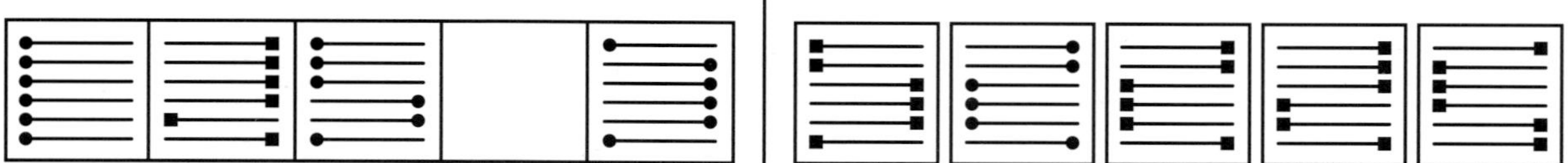

a b c d e

Score

Section D

The following figures correspond to the codes next to them. You must decide how the code letters go with the figures and then find the correct code for the Test Figure.

Example

 AZ

 BZ

 CY

TEST FIGURE

CZ	BY	AY	BZ	AZ
a	**b**	**(c)**	**d**	**e**

Now do the questions below. Circle the correct answer.

1)

 FL

 GM

 GN

TEST FIGURE

GL	FN	GM	GN	FM
a	**b**	**c**	**d**	**e**

2)

 APX

 BQY

 CPY

TEST FIGURE

CPX	AQX	CQX	BQX	CQY
a	**b**	**c**	**d**	**e**

3)

 ES

 FT

 GU

 FS

TEST FIGURE

GT	ET	GS	EU	FU
a	**b**	**c**	**d**	**e**

4)

 WEA

 XFB

 XGA

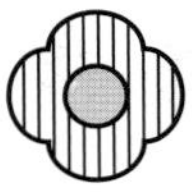
TEST FIGURE

WFA	XGA	WGB	XEB	WFB
a	**b**	**c**	**d**	**e**

5)

 JPA

 JQB

 KPB

TEST FIGURE

JQA	KPA	KQB	JPB	KQA
a	**b**	**c**	**d**	**e**

6)

 RLE

 SMF

 TNE

 SOF

TEST FIGURE

RNF	RNE	RMF	SNF	TNF
a	**b**	**c**	**d**	**e**

7)

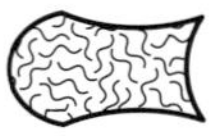 XAP

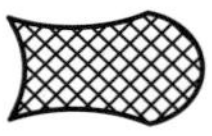 XBQ

 YCQ

 YAR

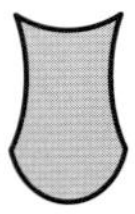
TEST FIGURE

XBR	XCR	YCR	XCP	XBP
a	**b**	**c**	**d**	**e**

8)

 ZAJP

 YAKQ

 XBLP

 ZCMQ

TEST FIGURE

YCKQ	YCLP	XCLQ	YCLQ	YBMQ
a	**b**	**c**	**d**	**e**

Score

Non-verbal Reasoning Test 7

Section A

The following figures correspond to the codes next to them. You must decide how the code letters go with the figures and then find the correct code for the Test Figure.

Example

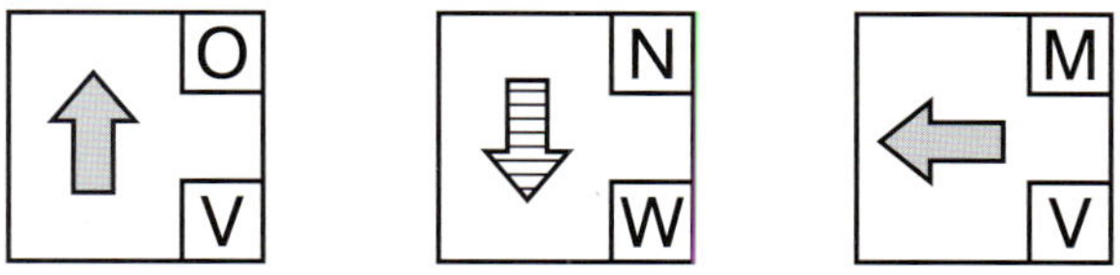

TEST FIGURE

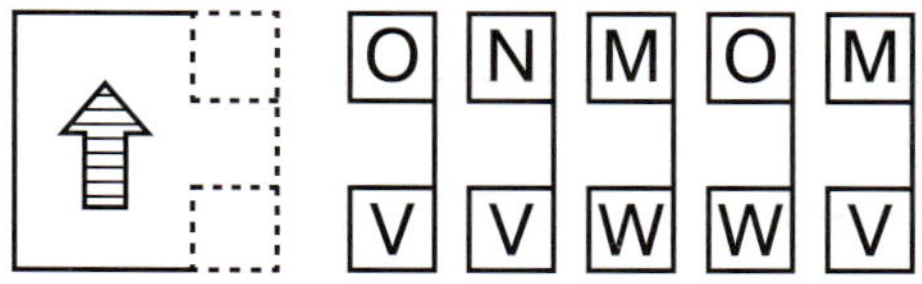

a b c (d circled) e

Now do the questions below. Circle the correct answer.

1)

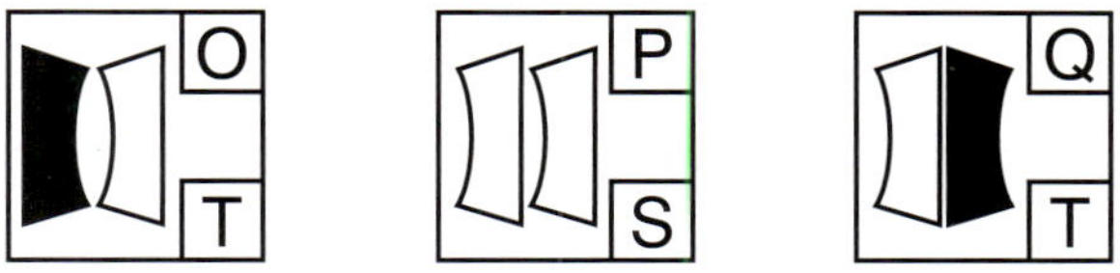

TEST FIGURE

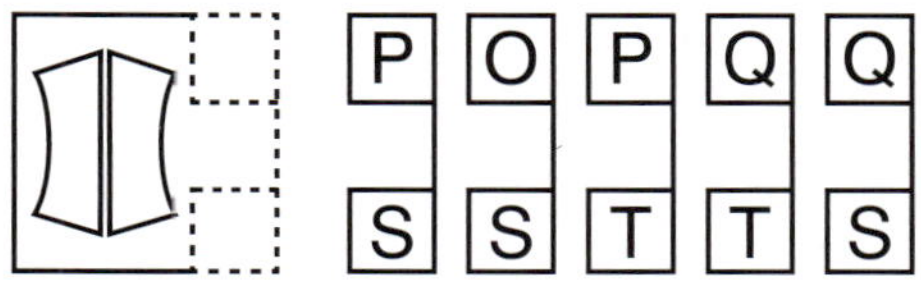

a b c d e

2)

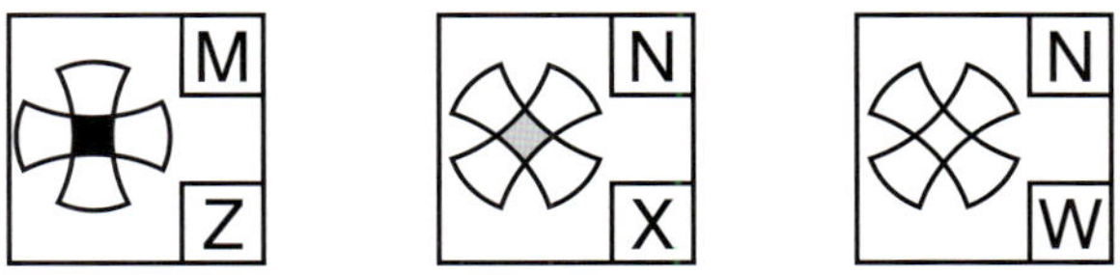

TEST FIGURE

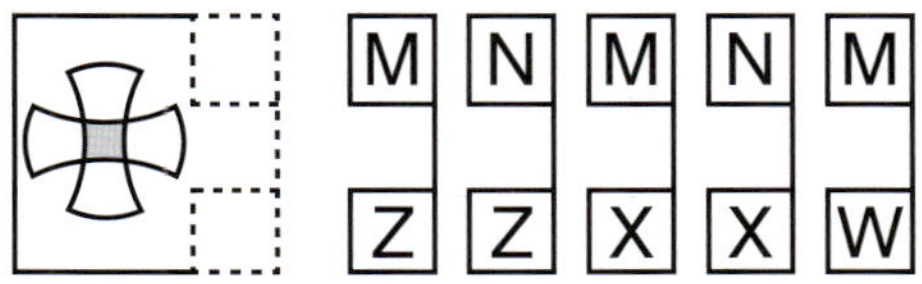

a b c d e

3)

TEST FIGURE

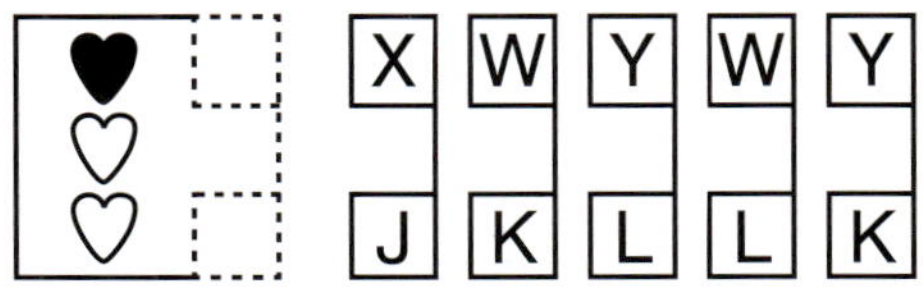

a b c d e

4)

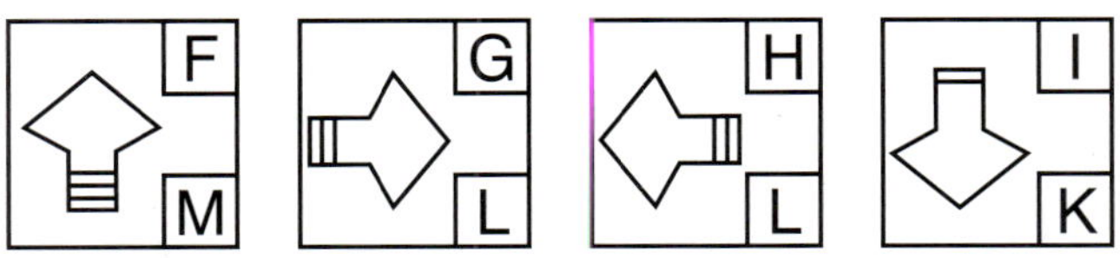

TEST FIGURE

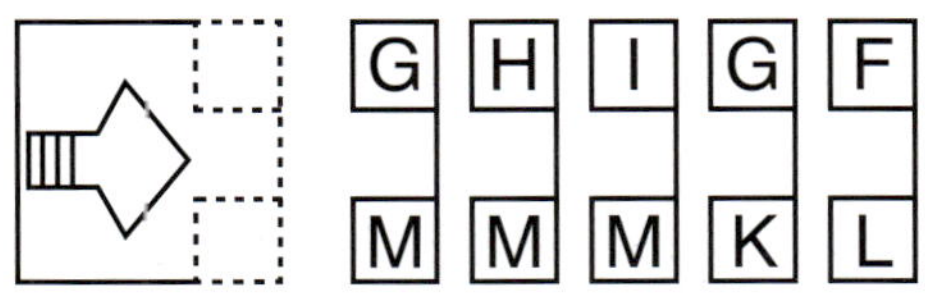

a b c d e

5)

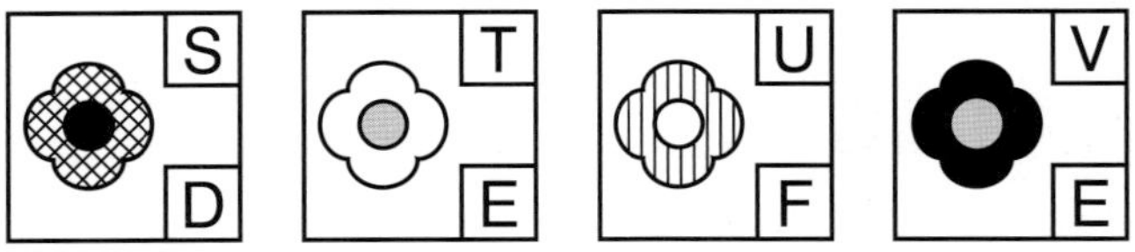

TEST FIGURE

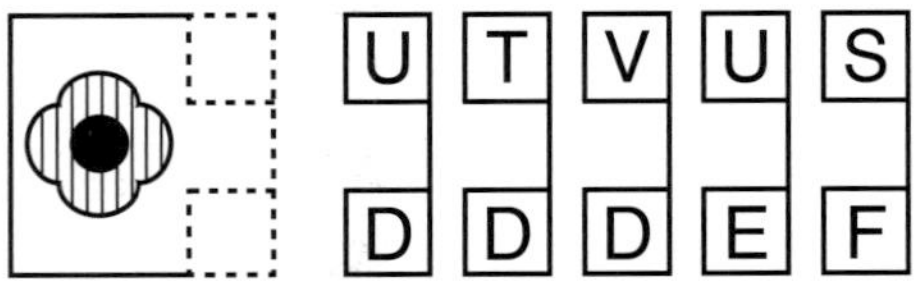

a b c d e

6)

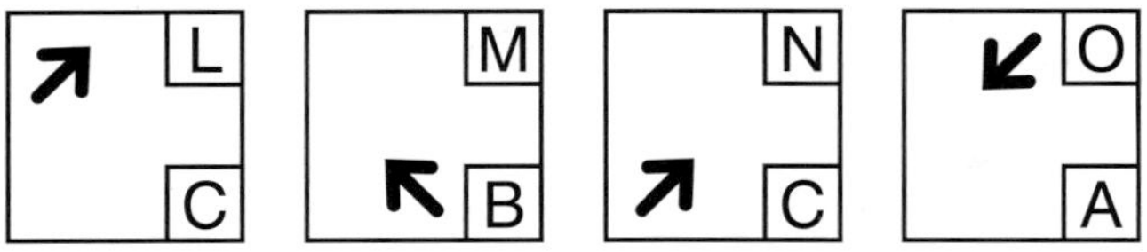

TEST FIGURE

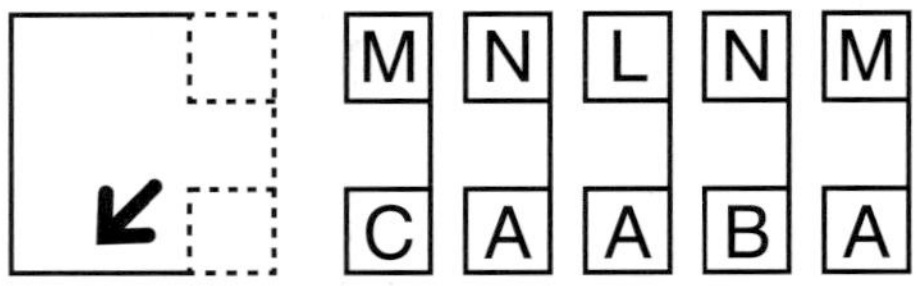

a b c d e

7)

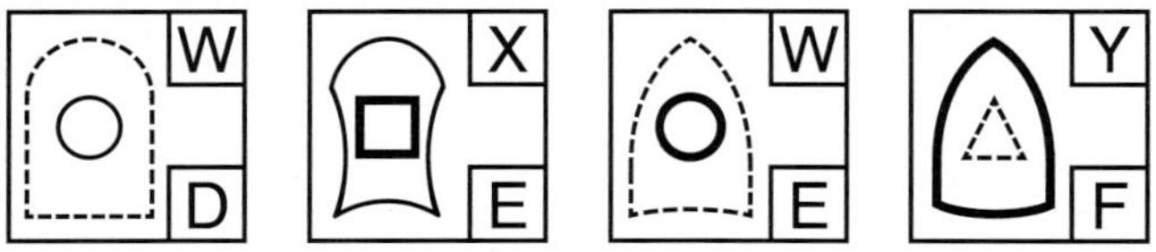

TEST FIGURE

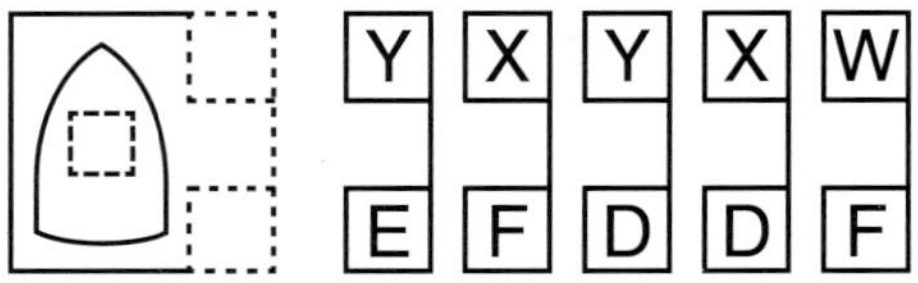

a b c d e

8)

TEST FIGURE

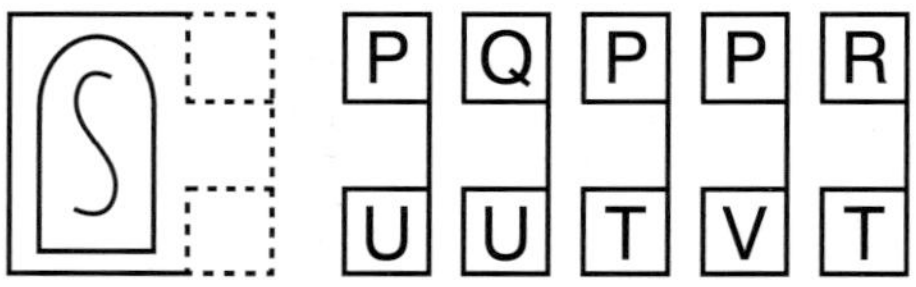

a b c d e

9)

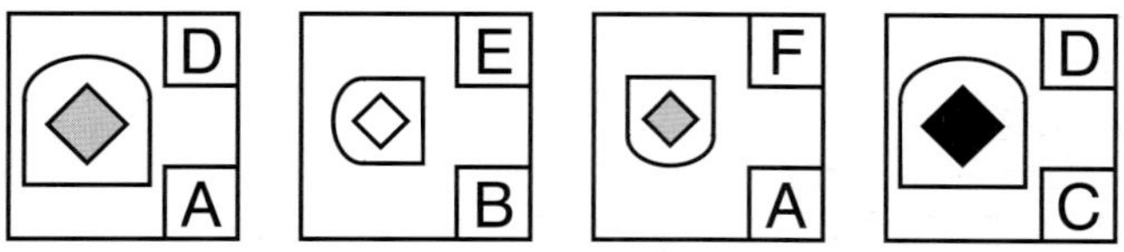

TEST FIGURE

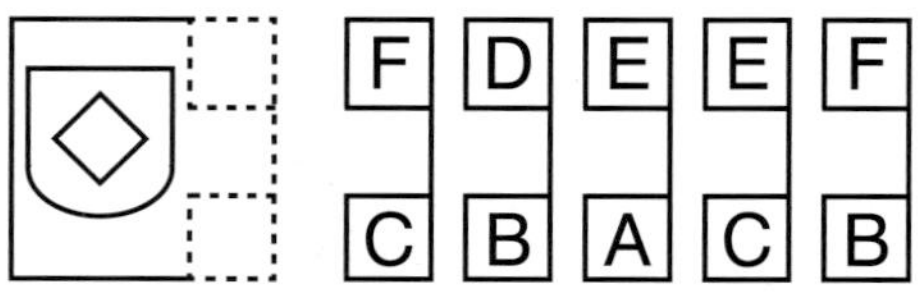

a b c d e

Score

Section B

On the left of each row are two figures with an arrow between them. Decide how the second figure is related to the first. After these there is a third figure, then an arrow and then five more figures. Decide which of the five figures goes with the third figure to make a pair like the two figures on the left.

Example

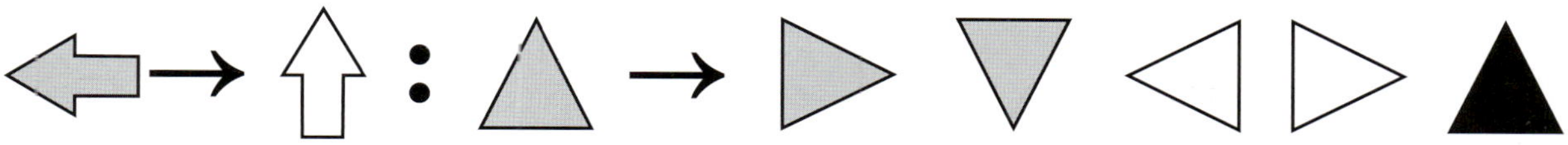

a b c (d) e

Now do the questions below. Circle the correct answer.

1)

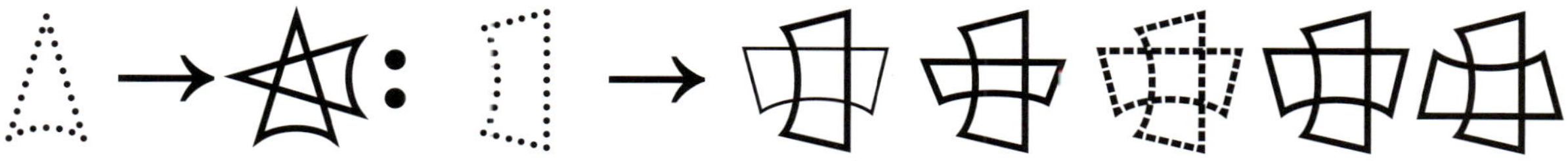

a b c d e

2)

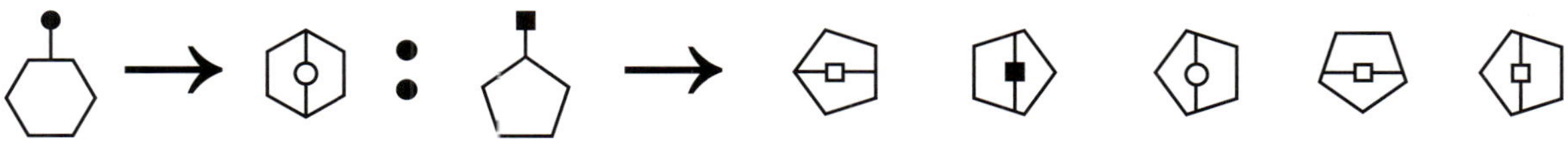

a b c d e

3)

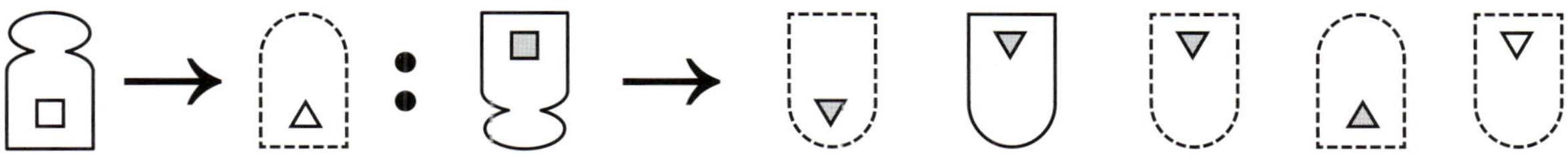

a b c d e

4)

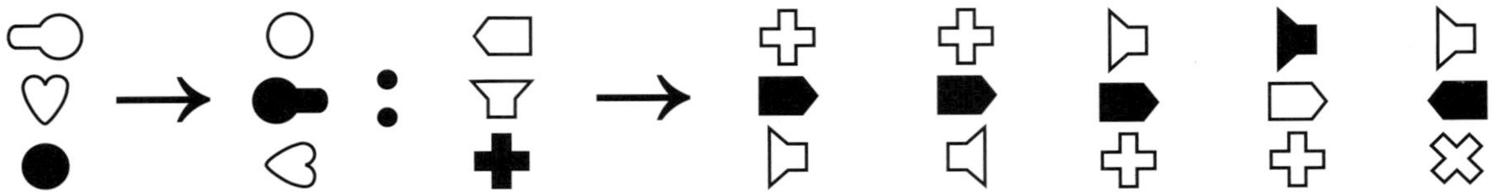

a b c d e

5)

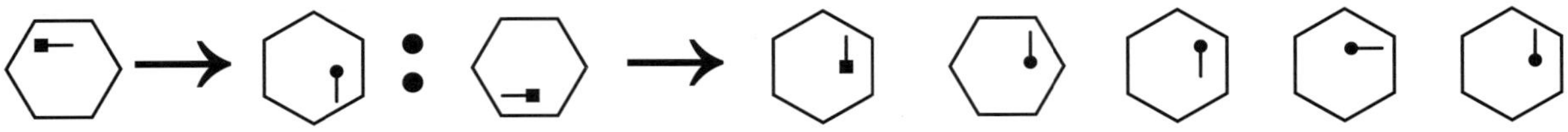

a b c d e

6)

a b c d e

7)

a b c d e

8)

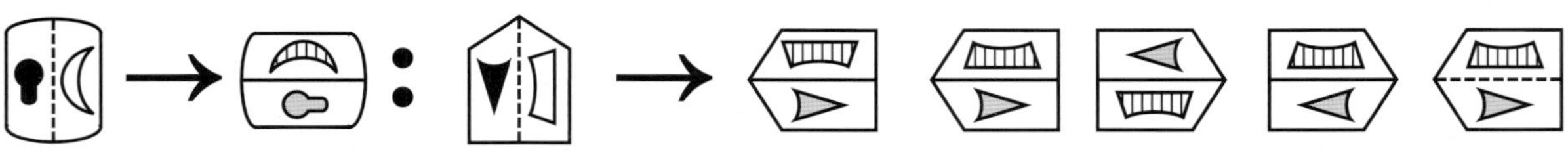

a b c d e

Score

Section C

In the big square on the left of each line below, one of the small squares has been left empty. One of the five figures on the right should fill the empty square. Find this figure.

Example

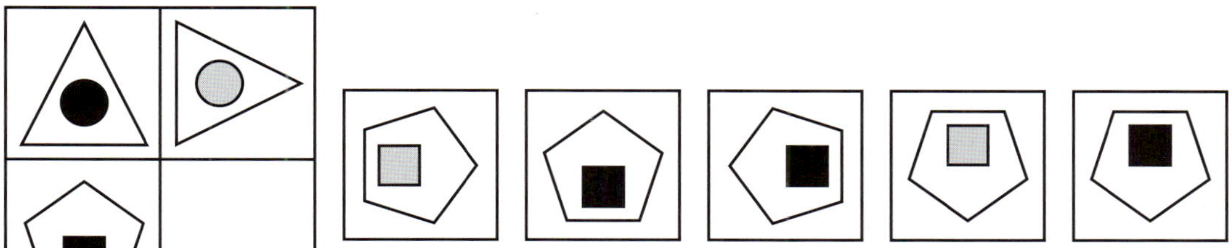

(a) b c d e

Now do the questions below. Circle the correct answer.

1)

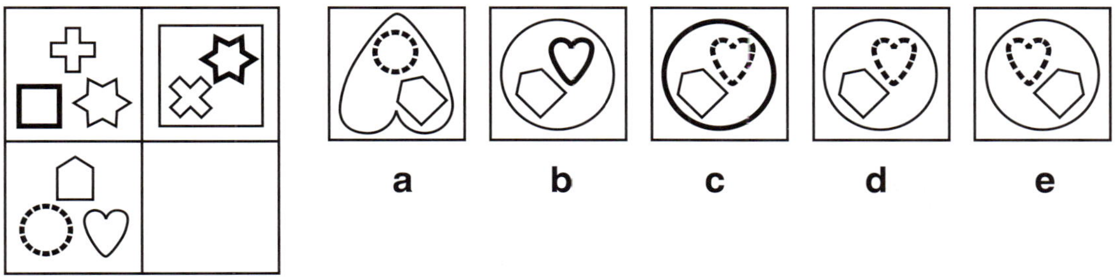

a b c d e

2)

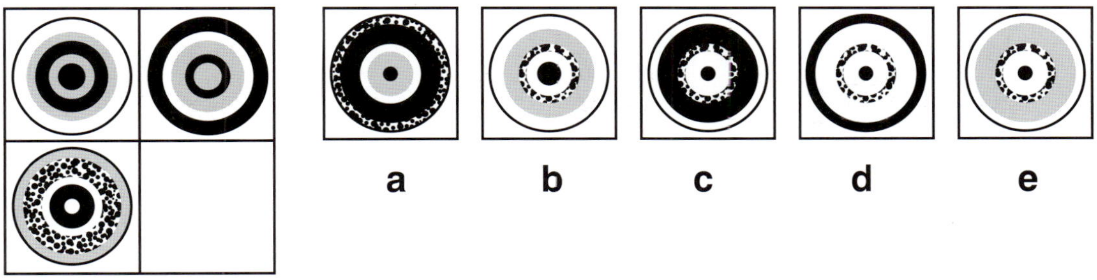

a b c d e

3)

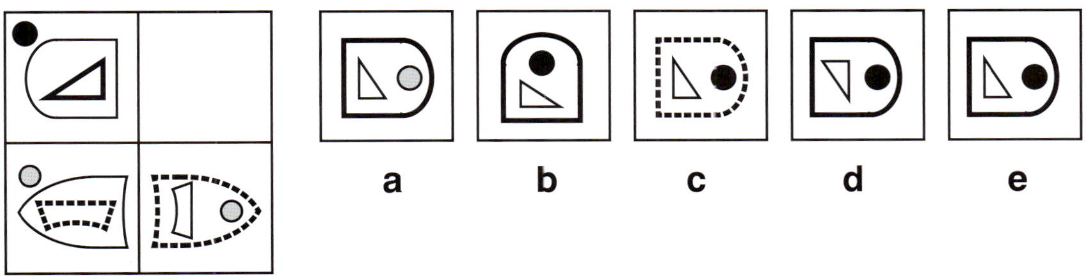

a b c d e

4)

a b c d e

5)

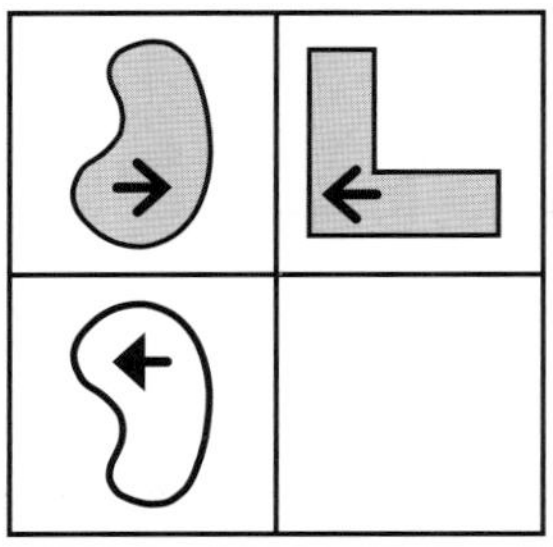

a b c d e

6)

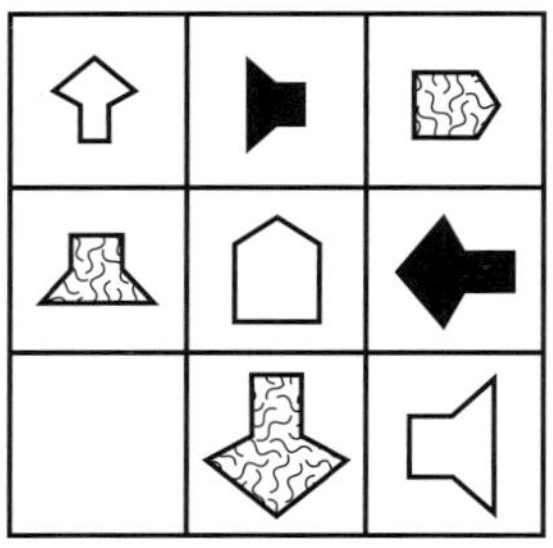

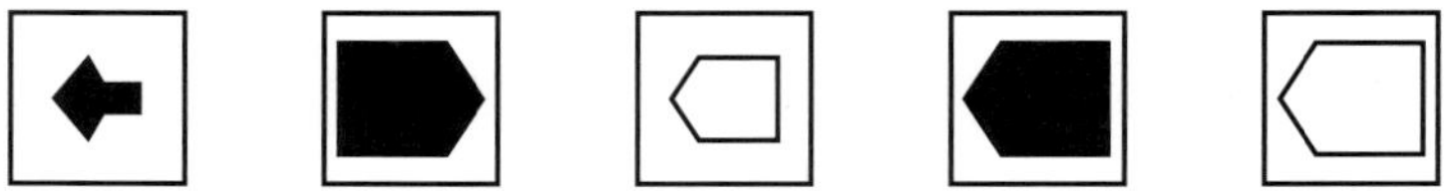

a b c d e

7)

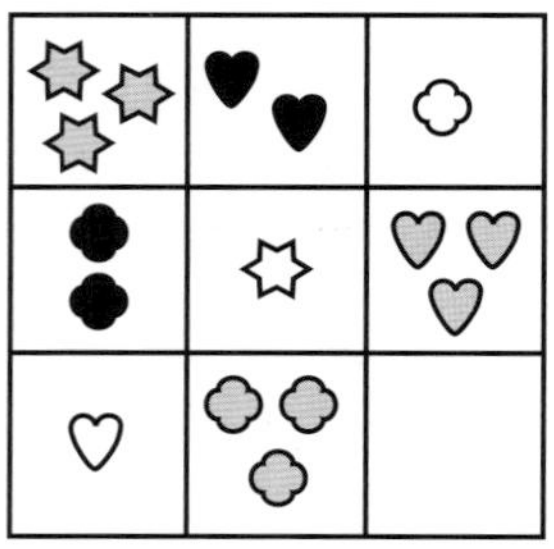

a b c d e

8)

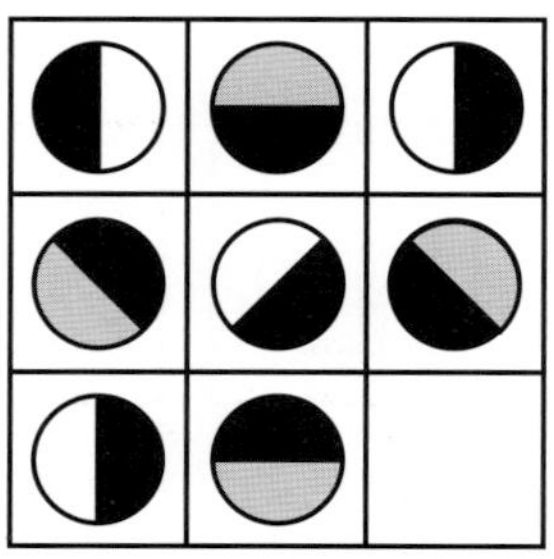

a b c d e

Score

Section D

On the left of each of the rows below there are two figures that are alike. On the right there are five more figures. Find which one of these five is **most like** the two figures on the left.

Example

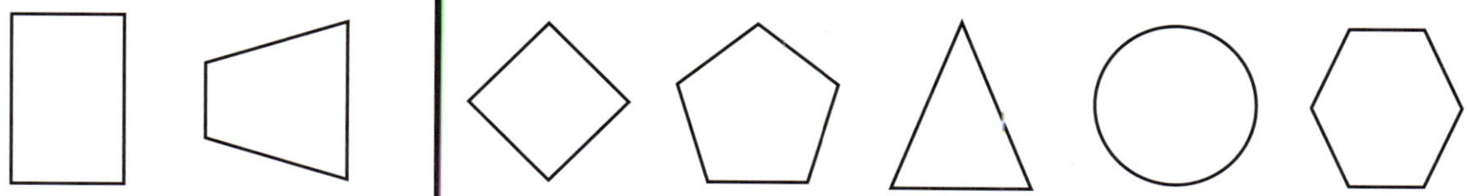

(a) b c d e

Now do the questions below. Circle the correct answer.

1)

a b c d e

2)

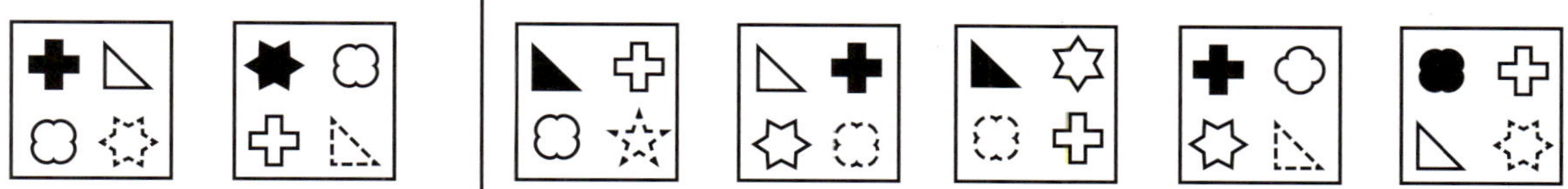

a b c d e

3)

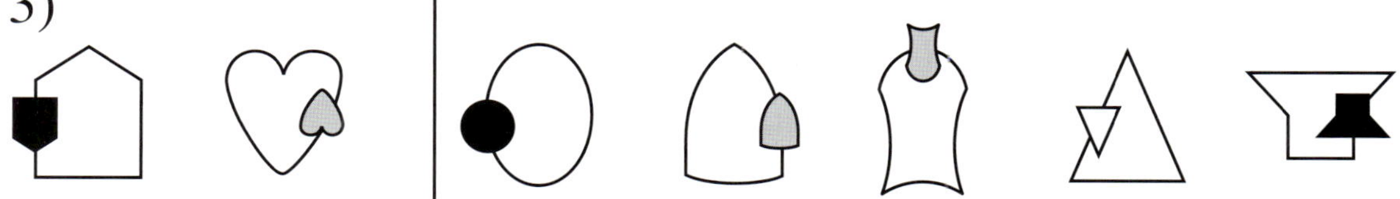

a b c d e

4)

a b c d e

5)

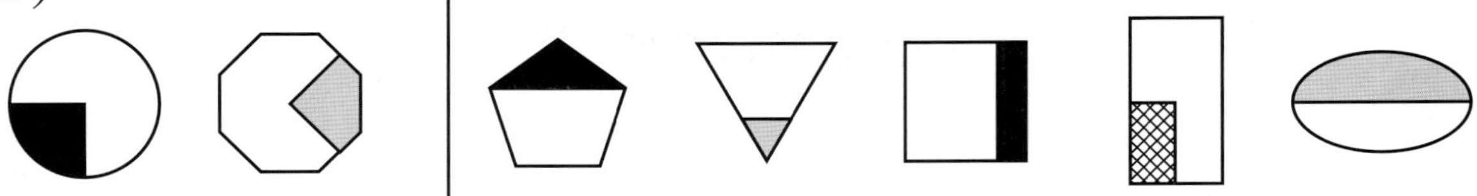

a b c d e

6)

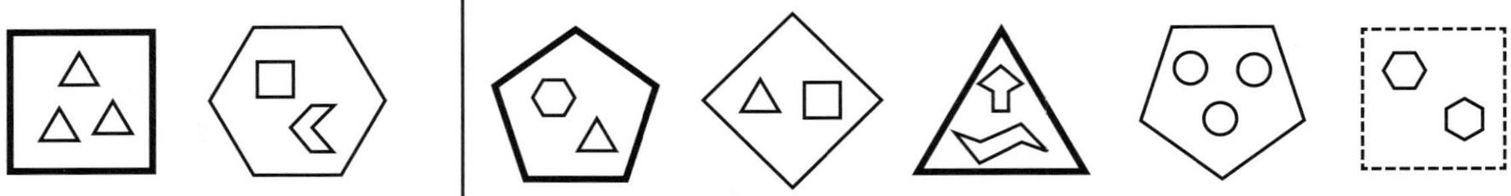

a b c d e

7)

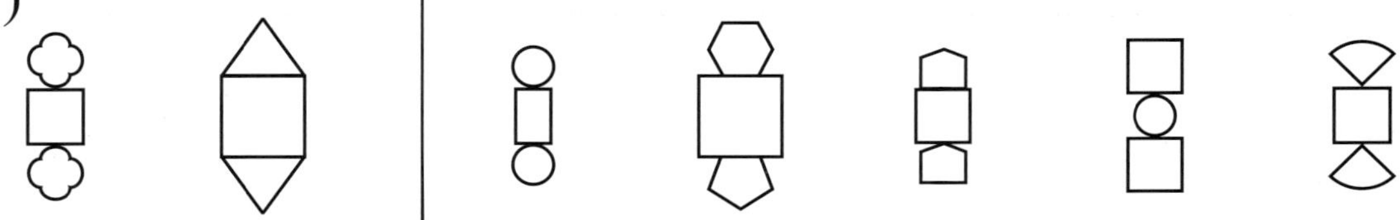

a b c d e

8)

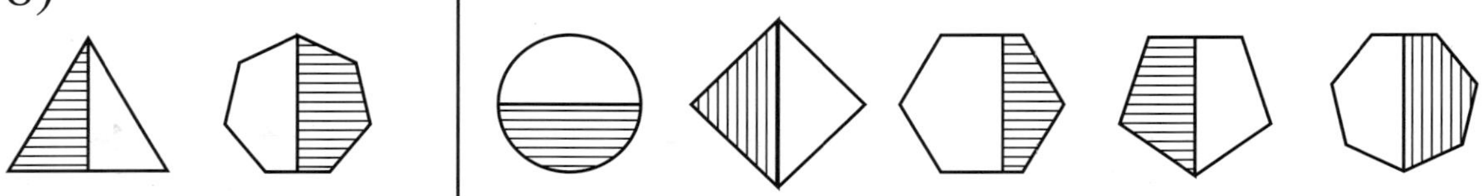

a b c d e

9)

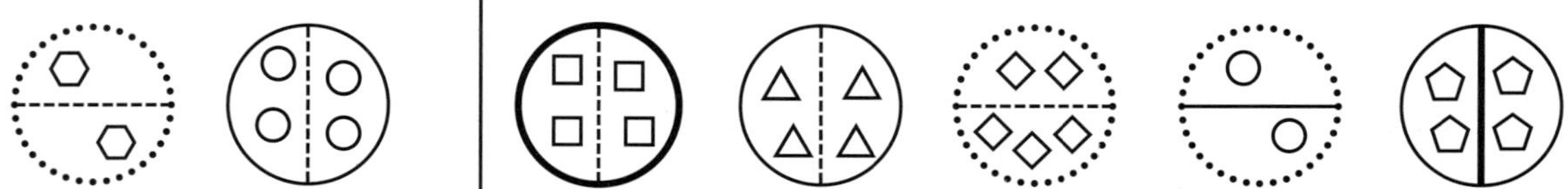

a b c d e

10)

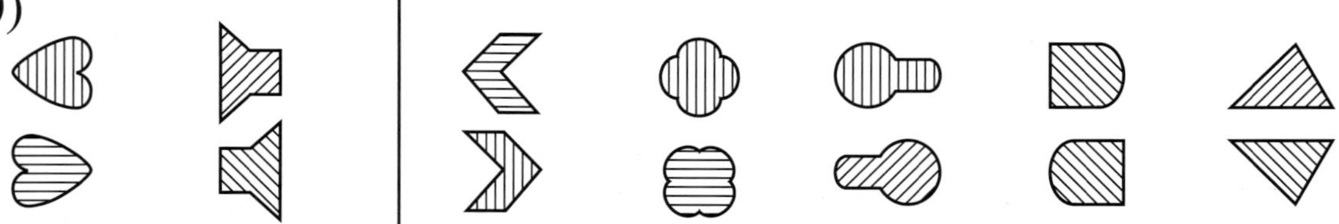

a b c d e

Score

Non-verbal Reasoning Test 8

Section A

On the left of each of the rows below there are two figures that are alike. On the right there are five more figures. Find which one of these five is **most like** the two figures on the left.

Example

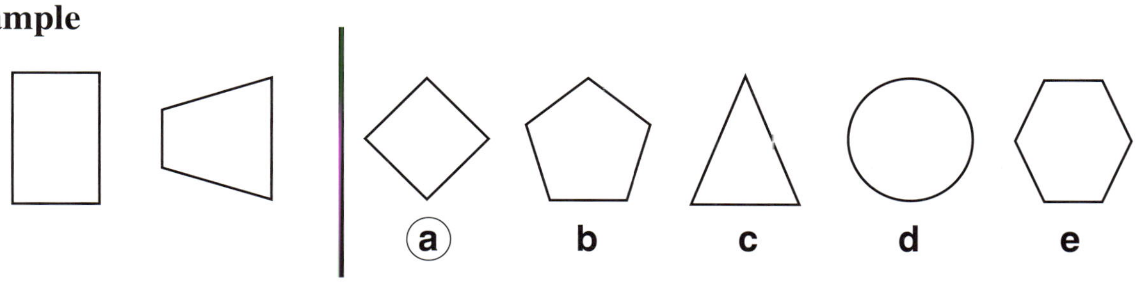

Now do the questions below. Circle the correct answer.

1)

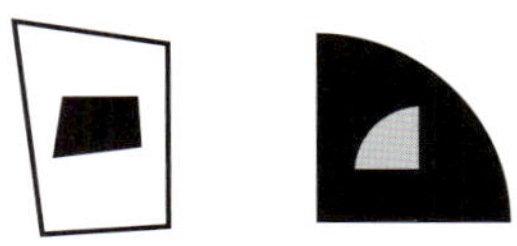

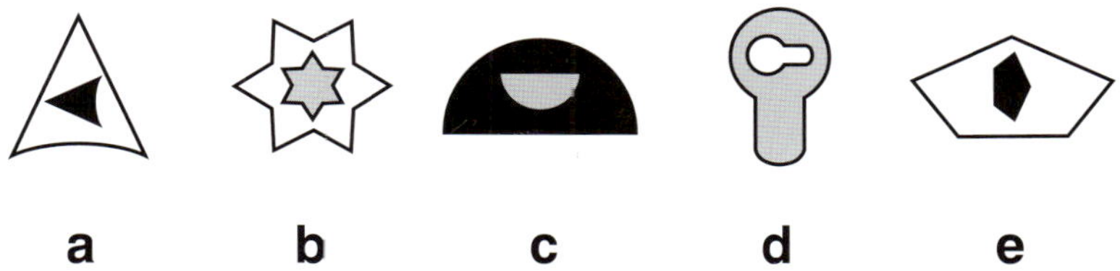

2)

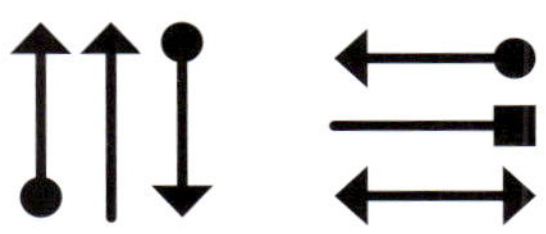

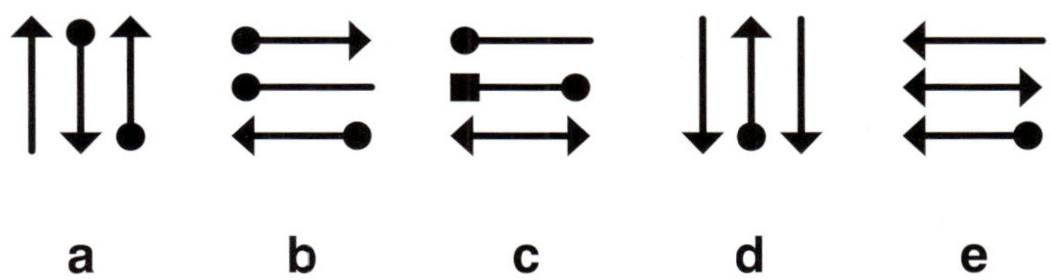

3)

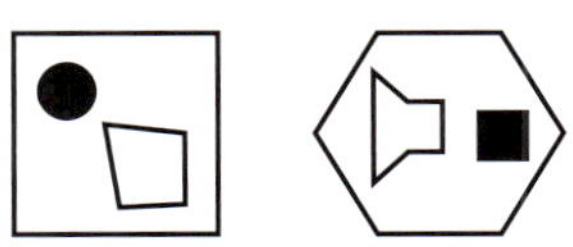

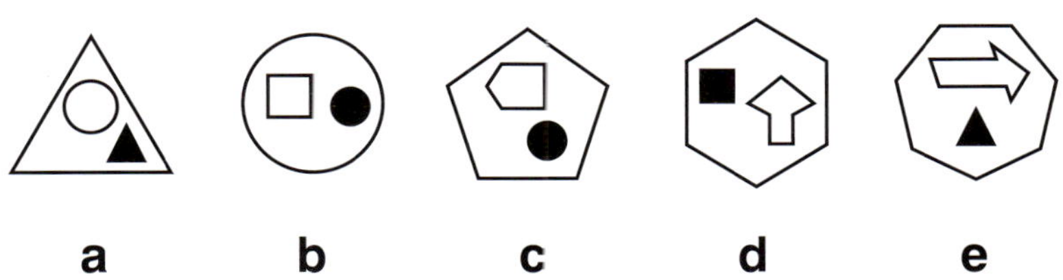

4)

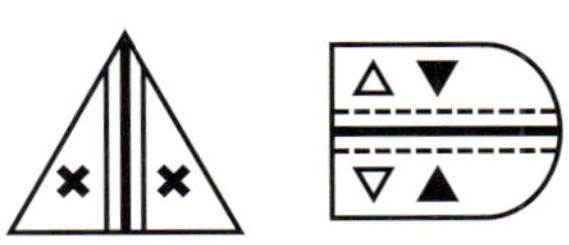

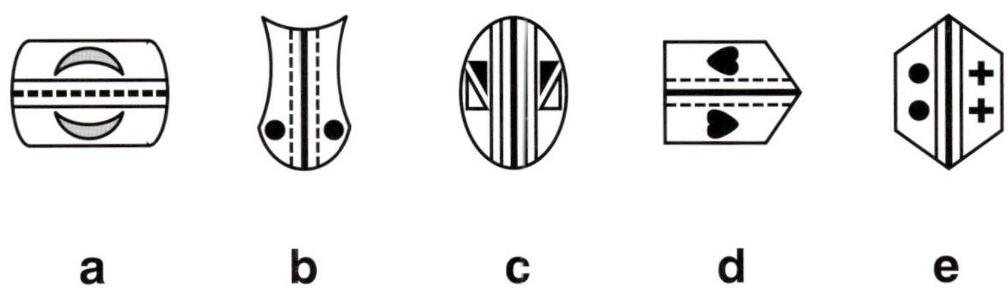

5)

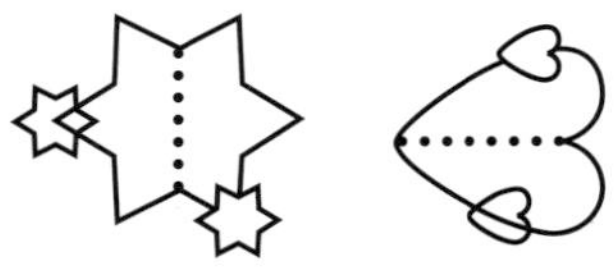

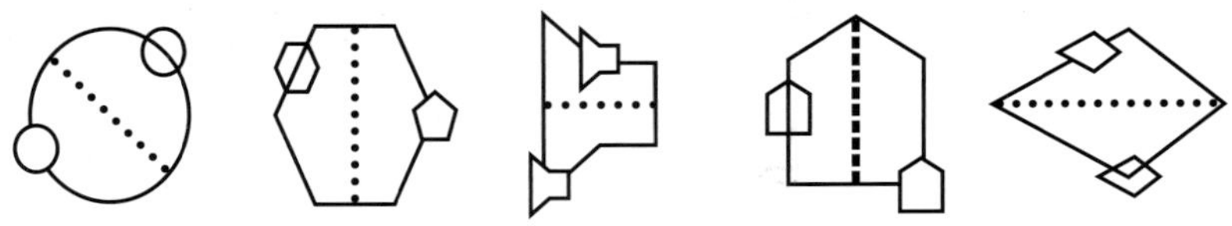

a b c d e

6)

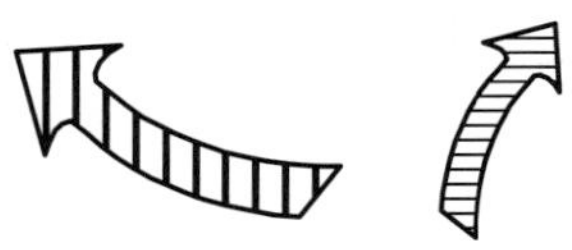

a b c d e

7)

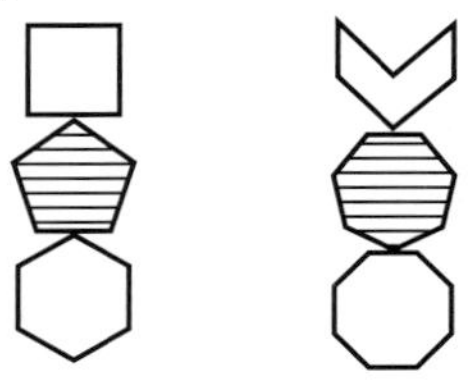

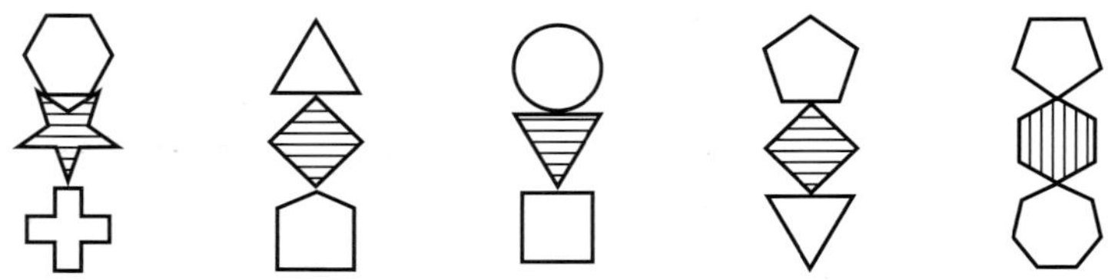

a b c d e

8)

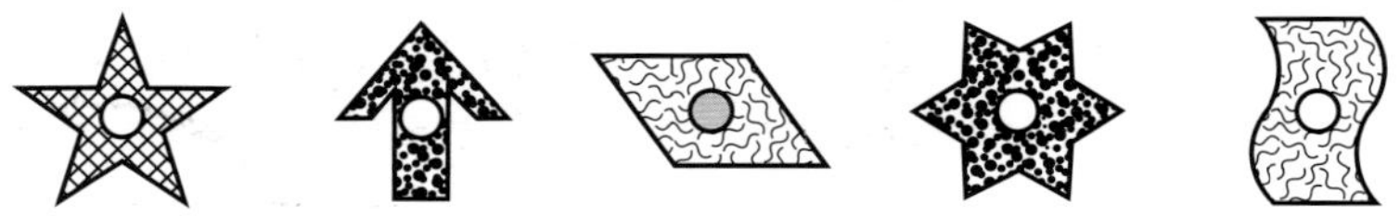

a b c d e

9)

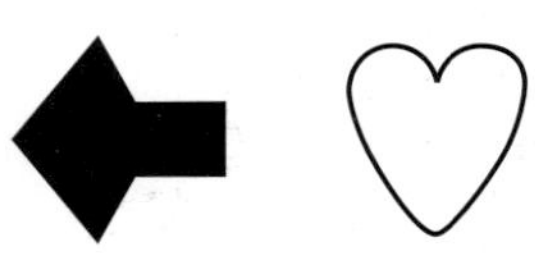

a b c d e

Score

Section B

To the left of each of the lines below there are five squares arranged in order. One of these squares has been left empty. Find which one of the five squares on the right should take the place of the empty square.

Example

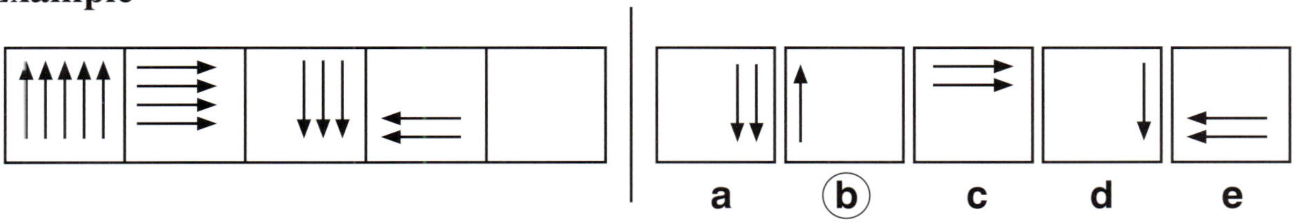

a (b) c d e

Now do the questions below. Circle the correct answer.

1)

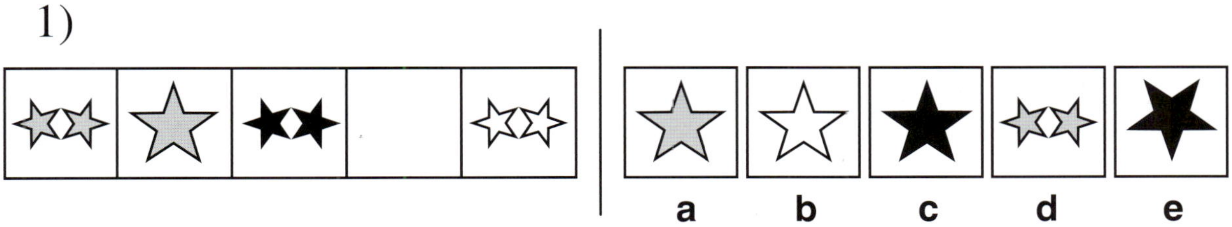

a b c d e

2)

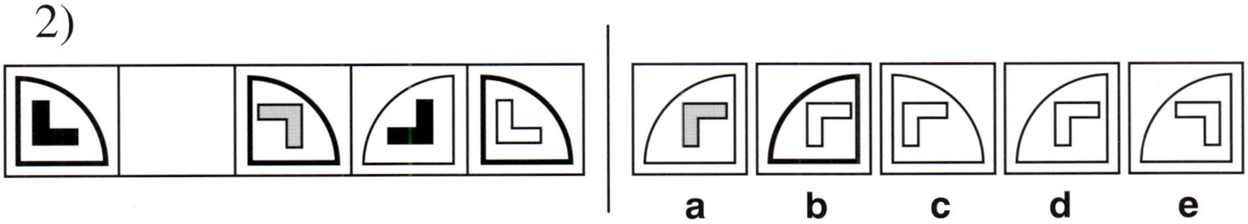

a b c d e

3)

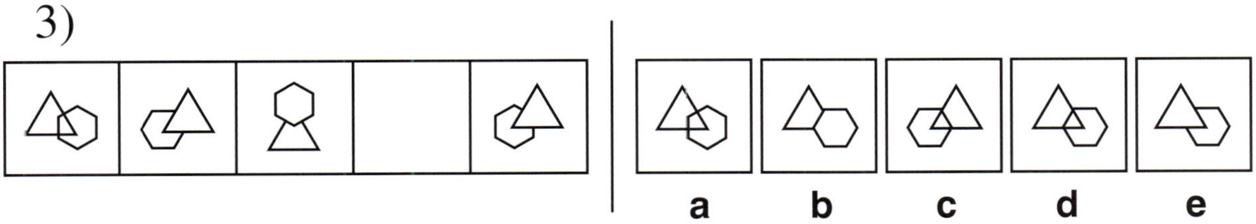

a b c d e

4)

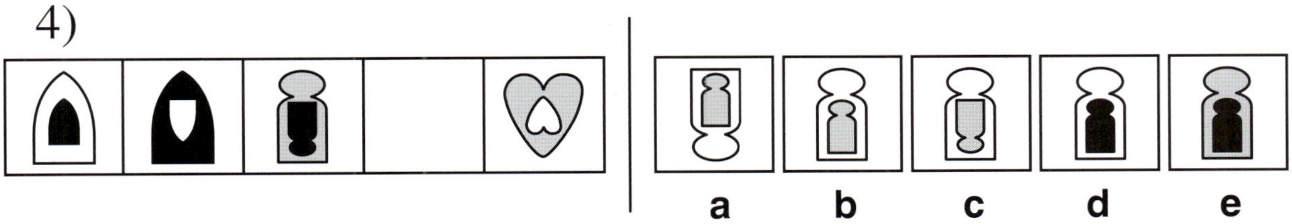

a b c d e

5)

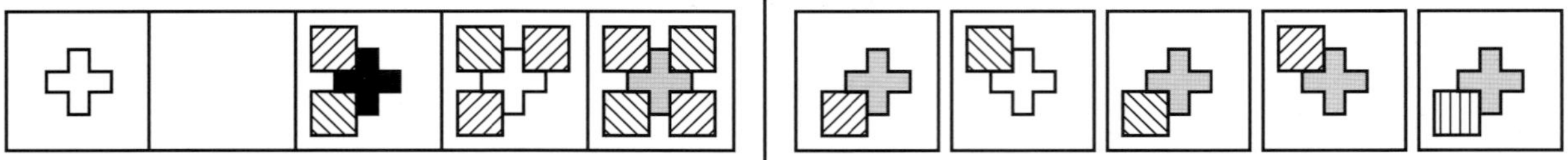

a b c d e

6)

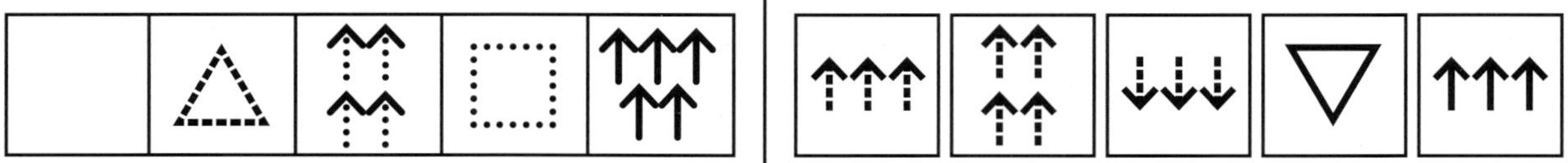

a b c d e

7)

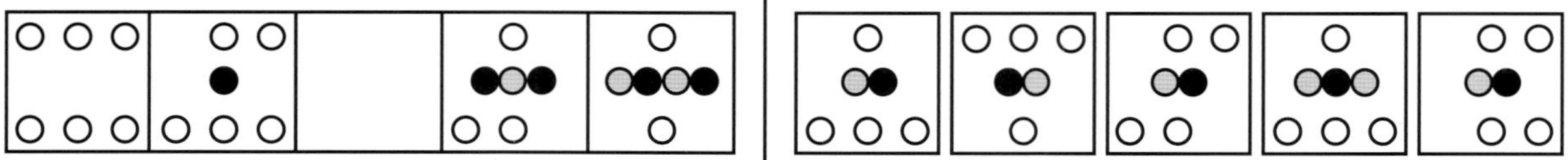

a b c d e

8)

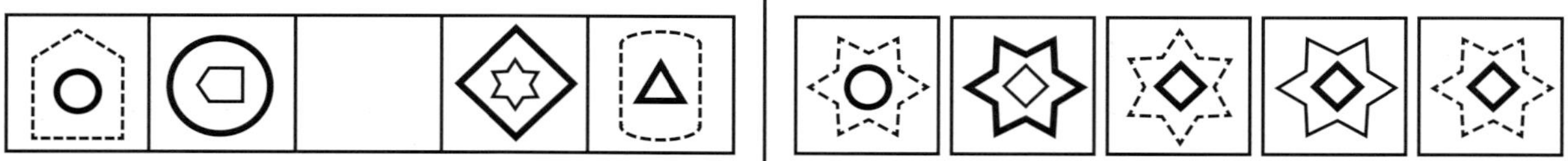

a b c d e

9)

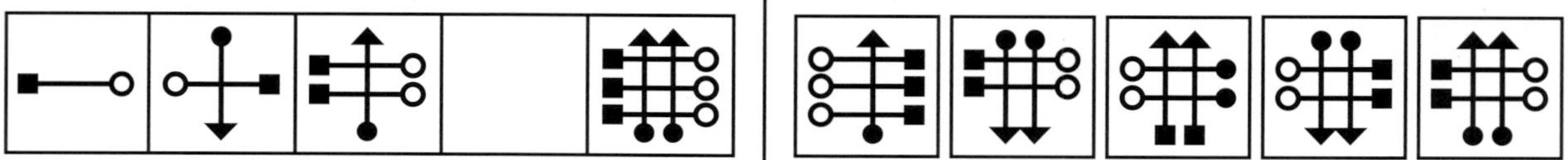

a b c d e

10)

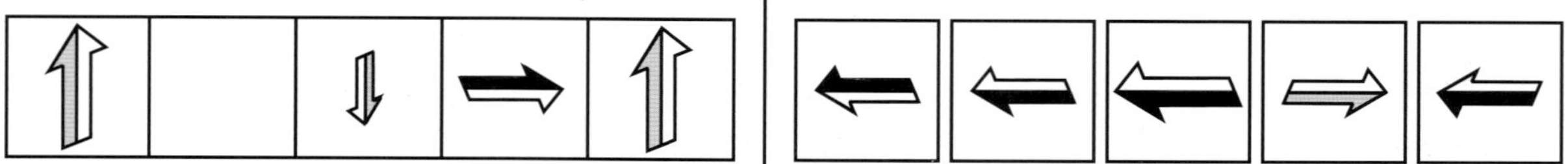

a b c d e

Score

Section C

In each of the rows below there are five figures. Find one figure in each row that is **most unlike** the other four.

Example

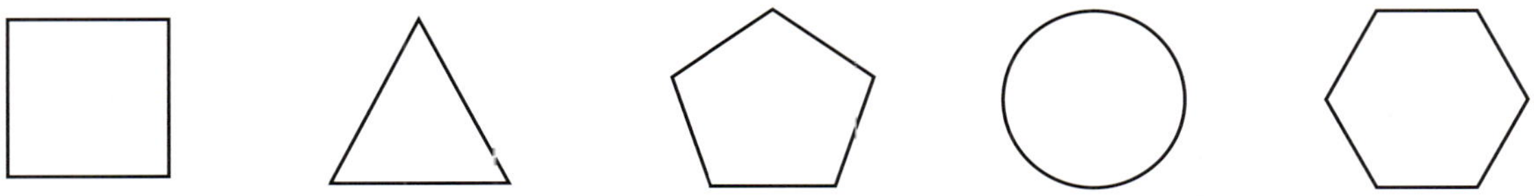

a b c d e

Now do the questions below. Circle the correct answer.

1)

a b c d e

2)

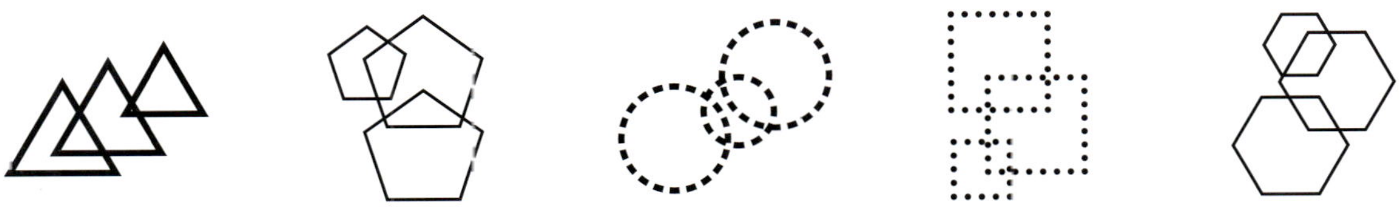

a b c d e

3)

a b c d e

4)

a b c d e

5)

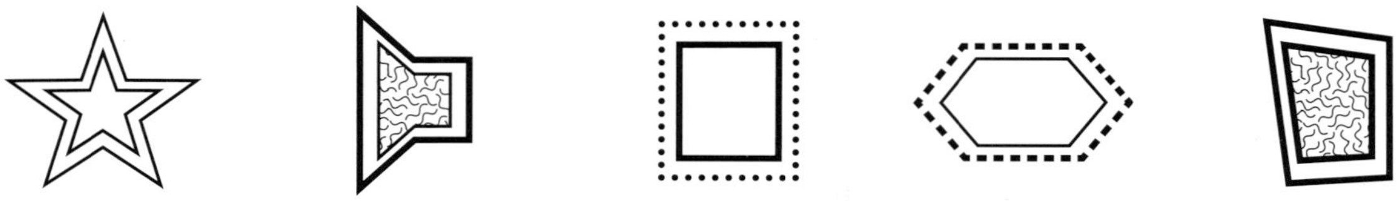

a b c d e

6)

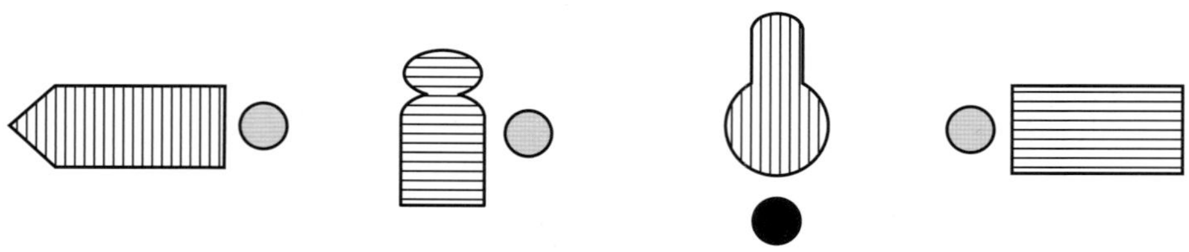

a b c d e

7)

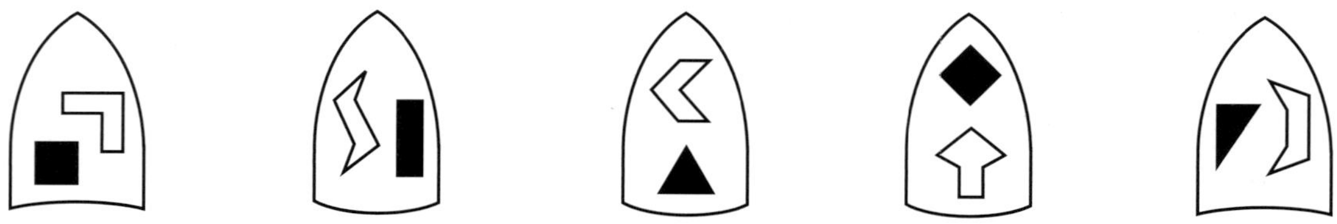

a b c d e

8)

a b c d e

Score

Section D

The following figures correspond to the codes next to them. You must decide how the code letters go with the figures and then find the correct code for the Test Figure.

Example

TEST FIGURE

CZ	BY	AY	BZ	AZ
a	**b**	**(c)**	**d**	**e**

Now do the questions below. Circle the correct answer.

1)

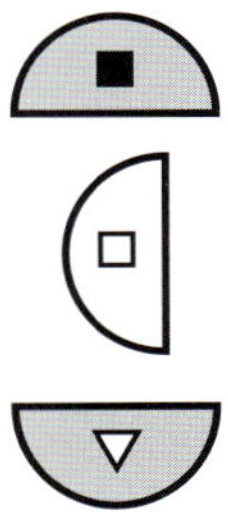

TEST FIGURE

SM	RN	RM	TM	TR
a	**b**	**c**	**d**	**e**

2)

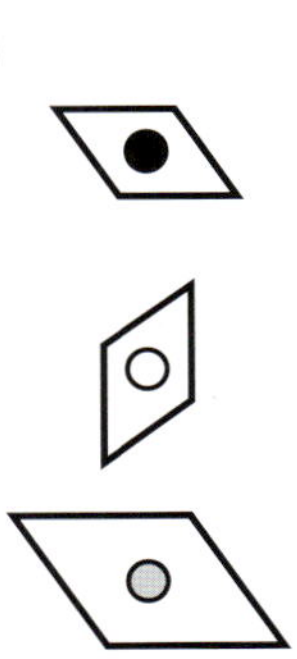

TEST FIGURE

PLG	QJG	QKG	QJF	QLG
a	**b**	**c**	**d**	**e**

3)

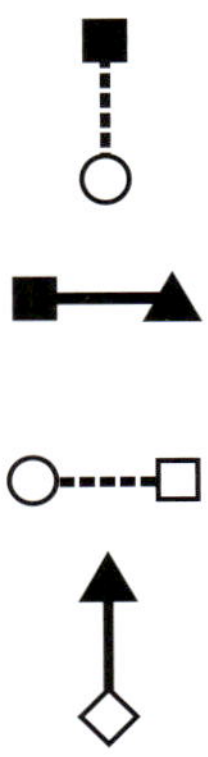

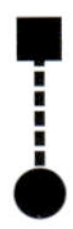

TEST FIGURE

XMS	YMS	XMT	YNT	XNS
a	**b**	**c**	**d**	**e**

4) 

ASE

BTF

ATG

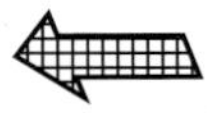

TEST FIGURE

ASG	ASF	BSE	BSG	BTG
a	**b**	**c**	**d**	**e**

5) 

XLP

YLQ

XMR

TEST FIGURE

YMR	XMP	XLQ	YMP	XLR
a	**b**	**c**	**d**	**e**

6) 

PAL

QBM

PCN

RAM

TEST FIGURE

PBL	RBL	RBM	QBL	RCL
a	**b**	**c**	**d**	**e**

7) 

AJXD

BKYE

ALZE

BKXD

TEST FIGURE

ALYD	BJYD	BLYD	BLZD	BLYE
a	**b**	**c**	**d**	**e**

8) 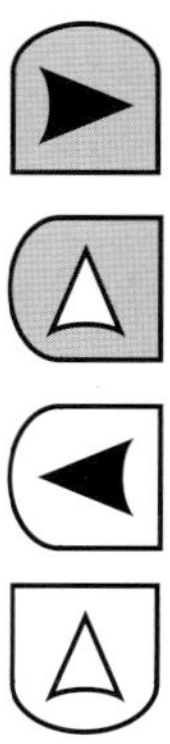

DNAF

DOBG

ENBH

EOCG

TEST FIGURE

DNCG	DNCH	DOCG	DNAG	ENCG
a	**b**	**c**	**d**	**e**

Score

Multiple-choice Answer Sheet
11+ Non-verbal Reasoning Year 5-7 Testbook 3

Test 1

Section A

EXAMPLE: a ▭ b ▬ c ▭ d ▭ e ▭

1: a b c d e
2: a b c d e
3: a b c d e
4: a b c d e
5: a b c d e
6: a b c d e
7: a b c d e
8: a b c d e
9: a b c d e

Section B

EXAMPLE: a ▬ b ▭ c ▭ d ▭ e ▭

1: a b c d e
2: a b c d e
3: a b c d e
4: a b c d e
5: a b c d e
6: a b c d e
7: a b c d e
8: a b c d e

Section C

EXAMPLE: a ▭ b ▭ c ▭ d ▬ e ▭

1: a b c d e
2: a b c d e
3: a b c d e
4: a b c d e
5: a b c d e
6: a b c d e
7: a b c d e
8: a b c d e

Section D

EXAMPLE: a ▭ b ▭ c ▭ d ▬ e ▭

1: a b c d e
2: a b c d e
3: a b c d e
4: a b c d e
5: a b c d e
6: a b c d e
7: a b c d e
8: a b c d e
9: a b c d e
10: a b c d e

Multiple-choice Answer Sheet
11+ Non-verbal Reasoning Year 5-7 Testbook 3

Test 2

Section A

EXAMPLE: a, b, c, d (marked), e

1: a b c d e
2: a b c d e
3: a b c d e
4: a b c d e
5: a b c d e
6: a b c d e
7: a b c d e
8: a b c d e

Section B

EXAMPLE: a, b, c, d (marked), e

1: a b c d e
2: a b c d e
3: a b c d e
4: a b c d e
5: a b c d e
6: a b c d e
7: a b c d e
8: a b c d e
9: a b c d e

Section C

EXAMPLE: a, b, c (marked), d, e

1: a b c d e
2: a b c d e
3: a b c d e
4: a b c d e
5: a b c d e
6: a b c d e
7: a b c d e
8: a b c d e

Section D

EXAMPLE: a (marked), b, c, d, e

1: a b c d e
2: a b c d e
3: a b c d e
4: a b c d e
5: a b c d e
6: a b c d e
7: a b c d e
8: a b c d e
9: a b c d e
10: a b c d e

Multiple-choice Answer Sheet
11+ Non-verbal Reasoning Year 5-7 Testbook 3

Test 3

Section A

EXAMPLE: a ▭ b ▭ c ▭ d ▬ e ▭

1 a b c d e
2 a b c d e
3 a b c d e
4 a b c d e
5 a b c d e
6 a b c d e
7 a b c d e
8 a b c d e
9 a b c d e

Section B

EXAMPLE: a ▬ b ▭ c ▭ d ▭ e ▭

1 a b c d e
2 a b c d e
3 a b c d e
4 a b c d e
5 a b c d e
6 a b c d e
7 a b c d e
8 a b c d e

Section C

EXAMPLE: a ▭ b ▬ c ▭ d ▭ e ▭

1 a b c d e
2 a b c d e
3 a b c d e
4 a b c d e
5 a b c d e
6 a b c d e
7 a b c d e
8 a b c d e
9 a b c d e
10 a b c d e

Section D

EXAMPLE: a ▭ b ▭ c ▭ d ▬ e ▭

1 a b c d e
2 a b c d e
3 a b c d e
4 a b c d e
5 a b c d e
6 a b c d e
7 a b c d e
8 a b c d e

Multiple-choice Answer Sheet
11+ Non-verbal Reasoning Year 5-7 Testbook 3

Test 4

Section A

EXAMPLE: a b c d e

1: a b c d e
2: a b c d e
3: a b c d e
4: a b c d e
5: a b c d e
6: a b c d e
7: a b c d e
8: a b c d e
9: a b c d e

Section B

EXAMPLE: a b c d e

1: a b c d e
2: a b c d e
3: a b c d e
4: a b c d e
5: a b c d e
6: a b c d e
7: a b c d e
8: a b c d e

Section C

EXAMPLE: a b c d e

1: a b c d e
2: a b c d e
3: a b c d e
4: a b c d e
5: a b c d e
6: a b c d e
7: a b c d e
8: a b c d e

Section D

EXAMPLE: a b c d e

1: a b c d e
2: a b c d e
3: a b c d e
4: a b c d e
5: a b c d e
6: a b c d e
7: a b c d e
8: a b c d e
9: a b c d e
10: a b c d e

Multiple-choice Answer Sheet
11+ Non-verbal Reasoning Year 5-7 Testbook 3
Test 5

Section A

EXAMPLE: a, b (marked), c, d, e

1: a b c d e
2: a b c d e
3: a b c d e
4: a b c d e
5: a b c d e
6: a b c d e
7: a b c d e
8: a b c d e
9: a b c d e

Section B

EXAMPLE: a, b, c, d (marked), e

1: a b c d e
2: a b c d e
3: a b c d e
4: a b c d e
5: a b c d e
6: a b c d e
7: a b c d e
8: a b c d e

Section C

EXAMPLE: a, b, c, d (marked), e

1: a b c d e
2: a b c d e
3: a b c d e
4: a b c d e
5: a b c d e
6: a b c d e
7: a b c d e
8: a b c d e

Section D

EXAMPLE: a, b, c, d (marked), e

1: a b c d e
2: a b c d e
3: a b c d e
4: a b c d e
5: a b c d e
6: a b c d e
7: a b c d e
8: a b c d e
9: a b c d e
10: a b c d e

Multiple-choice Answer Sheet
11+ Non-verbal Reasoning Year 5-7 Testbook 3

Test 6

Section A

EXAMPLE: a (marked), b, c, d, e

1: a, b, c, d, e
2: a, b, c, d, e
3: a, b, c, d, e
4: a, b, c, d, e
5: a, b, c, d, e
6: a, b, c, d, e
7: a, b, c, d, e
8: a, b, c, d, e
9: a, b, c, d, e

Section B

EXAMPLE: a (marked), b, c, d, e

1: a, b, c, d, e
2: a, b, c, d, e
3: a, b, c, d, e
4: a, b, c, d, e
5: a, b, c, d, e
6: a, b, c, d, e
7: a, b, c, d, e
8: a, b, c, d, e

Section C

EXAMPLE: a, b (marked), c, d, e

1: a, b, c, d, e
2: a, b, c, d, e
3: a, b, c, d, e
4: a, b, c, d, e
5: a, b, c, d, e
6: a, b, c, d, e
7: a, b, c, d, e
8: a, b, c, d, e
9: a, b, c, d, e
10: a, b, c, d, e

Section D

EXAMPLE: a, b, c (marked), d, e

1: a, b, c, d, e
2: a, b, c, d, e
3: a, b, c, d, e
4: a, b, c, d, e
5: a, b, c, d, e
6: a, b, c, d, e
7: a, b, c, d, e
8: a, b, c, d, e

Multiple-choice Answer Sheet
11+ Non-verbal Reasoning Year 5-7 Testbook 3

Test 7

Section A

EXAMPLE: a b c d e

1: a b c d e
2: a b c d e
3: a b c d e
4: a b c d e
5: a b c d e
6: a b c d e
7: a b c d e
8: a b c d e
9: a b c d e

Section B

EXAMPLE: a b c d e

1: a b c d e
2: a b c d e
3: a b c d e
4: a b c d e
5: a b c d e
6: a b c d e
7: a b c d e
8: a b c d e

Section C

EXAMPLE: a b c d e

1: a b c d e
2: a b c d e
3: a b c d e
4: a b c d e
5: a b c d e
6: a b c d e
7: a b c d e
8: a b c d e

Section D

EXAMPLE: a b c d e

1: a b c d e
2: a b c d e
3: a b c d e
4: a b c d e
5: a b c d e
6: a b c d e
7: a b c d e
8: a b c d e
9: a b c d e
10: a b c d e

Multiple-choice Answer Sheet
11+ Non-verbal Reasoning Year 5-7 Testbook 3

Test 8

Section A

EXAMPLE: a (marked), b, c, d, e

1: a b c d e
2: a b c d e
3: a b c d e
4: a b c d e
5: a b c d e
6: a b c d e
7: a b c d e
8: a b c d e
9: a b c d e

Section B

EXAMPLE: a, b (marked), c, d, e

1: a b c d e
2: a b c d e
3: a b c d e
4: a b c d e
5: a b c d e
6: a b c d e
7: a b c d e
8: a b c d e
9: a b c d e
10: a b c d e

Section C

EXAMPLE: a, b, c, d (marked), e

1: a b c d e
2: a b c d e
3: a b c d e
4: a b c d e
5: a b c d e
6: a b c d e
7: a b c d e
8: a b c d e

Section D

EXAMPLE: a, b, c (marked), d, e

1: a b c d e
2: a b c d e
3: a b c d e
4: a b c d e
5: a b c d e
6: a b c d e
7: a b c d e
8: a b c d e

Answers

Non-verbal Reasoning Test 1
Section A

Example - **b** - The figure rotates 90° clockwise. One Arrow is subtracted.

1) **d** - The number of Circles is: 1, 2, 3, 4, 1. The Circles move down one position.
2) **d** - The figure rotates 90° clockwise. The Thick Line moves one position outwards.
3) **b** - The figure rotates 90° anticlockwise. The enclosed shape is: Circle, Square, Triangle, Circle, Square.
4) **a** - The Arrow rotates 90° anticlockwise amd moves one corner clockwise. The order of Line Endings is: Open Arrow, Small Triangle, Long Triangle, Open Arrow, Small Triangle.
5) **d** - The Outline alternates between Dotted and Dashed. The order of outer shapes is: Pentagon, Circle, Hexagon, Pentagon, Circle. The order of fills is: Black, White, Grey, White, Black.
6) **a** - The outer shape of the previous figure becomes the enclosed shape of the next figure. The Lined Fill rotates 45° clockwise.
7) **a** - The Blade Shape flips vertically and its position order is: bottom, middle, top, middle, bottom. The position order of the Star is: left, middle, right, middle, left. The order of fills of the Star is: White, Black, Grey, White, Black.
8) **b** - The shapes move one position inwards. The Lined Fill alternates between Horizontal and Vertical.
9) **d** - The Heart Shape increases in size and rotates 90° clockwise. The outline alternates between Thick and Thin. The order of fills is: Grey, Lattice, Mottled, Grey, Lattice.

Section B

Example - **a** - Solved horizontally: The figure has been rotated 90° clockwise. The Black Fill has become Grey.

1) **a** - Solved vertically: The outer shape has been reflected across the horizontal mid-line of the matrix. The Black Fill has become Grey.
2) **d** - Solved vertically: One side has been added. The Fill has been rotated 90°.
3) **c** - Solved horizontally: The figure has been rotated 90° anticlockwise.
4) **e** - Solved vertically: The shape in the bottom right has become the outer shape and has taken on the outline of the Circle. Two duplicates of the bottom left shape have been added, and all three have been enclosed.
5) **c** - Solved horizontally: The shape has been rotated 90°. Replicas of the shape have been added to equal the number of its sides.
6) **b** - Solved horizontally or vertically: There must be one White Fill, one Black Fill and one Lattice Fill. There must be one Star, one Cigar Shape and one Cross.
7) **a** - Solved vertically: The Black and Grey Fills have been alternated. The Line has been moved 90° clockwise.
8) **a** - Solved horizontally: The figure has been rotated 90° clockwise. There must be one Black, one Grey and one Lined Fill.

Section C

Example - **d** - The figure is not Straight-edged.

1) **d** - The shape does not have six sides.
2) **c** - The enclosed Star is not the same size as the others.
3) **b** - There are not more Crosses than Arrows.
4) **b** - The overlaid shape is not a 90° anticlockwise rotation of the larger shape.
5) **e** - The figure is an inversion of the others, not a rotation.
6) **c** - There are not two shapes that are the same size.
7) **a** - The Line is attached to a point, not an indent or a side.
8) **a** - The enclosed shapes do not have one more side than the outer shape.

Section D

Example - **d** - O - Arrow points upwards; W - Horizontal Lined Fill

1) **d** - E - Thin Outline; T - 5-pointed Star

Answers

2) **d** - K - Circle Line Ending with a White Fill; X - Triangle points downwards
3) **a** - Q - Triangle; L - One shape
4) **a** - M - Smaller figure; X - Heart Shape points upwards
5) **b** - N - Bulb Shape faces upwards; H - Large figure
6) **e** - R - Grey and White Fills; B - Horizontal Figure
7) **b** - A - Circle has a Grey Fill; X - Cross has a Black Fill
8) **c** - F - Rectangle is on the bottom; Q - Hexagon
9) **d** - Y - Outer shape is a Square; K - Enclosed shape is a Circle
10) **a** - O - Eight Line Endings; C - Square Line Ending with a White Fill

Non-verbal Reasoning Test 2
Section A

Example - **d** - The figure rotates 90° clockwise. The fill becomes White.

1) **b** - The shape reduces in size. The White Fill becomes Grey.
2) **d** - The shapes swap.
3) **e** - The shape rotates 90° anticlockwise. The outline becomes thicker. The White Fill becomes Mottled.
4) **b** - The shape reduces. Replica shapes are added to equal the number of its sides. The White Fill becomes Black.
5) **b** - The shape is quartered. The Lined Fill is rotated 90°.
6) **d** - The figure on the left rotates 90° clockwise to become the top figure. The figure on the right rotates 90° anticlockwise to become the bottom figure.
7) **d** - The figure vertically flips. The enclosed Circle becomes a White Square with a Grey Square enclosed.
8) **e** - One side is added. The shape is enlarged. The Thin Solid Outline becomes Thick Dotted.

Section B

Example - **d** - The figure is not Straight-edged.

1) **d** - The enclosed shapes are not either a replica or a 90° anticlockwise rotation of the outer shape.
2) **d** - The two Circles that are the same size are not the smallest.
3) **c** - The shape does not have a Vertical or Horizontal Lined Fill.
4) **a** - The small shape is not a 180° rotation of the large shape.
5) **b** - The Flower Shape does not have a White Fill.
6) **d** - The outer shape is not Curved and the enclosed shape(s) is not Straight-edged.
7) **e** - The Arrow Line Ending is not closed.
8) **c** - The fill of the Triangle is not Horizontal Lined Fill.
9) **c** - The longest Line does not have a Square Line Ending.

Section C

Example - **c** - A - Circle; Y - Grey Fill

1) **e** - U - Chevron Shape points to the right; D - Mottled Fill
2) **c** - C - White Fill; Y - Semi-circle is Vertical; F - Square
3) **a** - M - White Fill; G - Plus Shape; P - Small shape
4) **b** - M - Star with point at the top; S - Enclosed shapes have horizontal orientation; P - Squares are enclosed
5) **a** - Q - Churn Shape has a White Fill; I - Outer shape is a House Shape; W - Churn Shape faces to the right
6) **c** - X - Dotted Line; B - Horizontal Line; S - Hexagon
7) **e** - S - One Circle with a Black Fill; P - Triangle points to the right; Z - Triangle has a White Fill
8) **d** - O - Two Heart Shapes; K - Heart Shapes point downwards; F - Outer Heart Shape has a Dashed Outline; T - Enclosed Circle has a Grey Fill

Section D

Example - **a** - The shape has four sides.

1) **b** - The shape does not have a line of symmetry and has a Black or Grey Fill.
2) **a** - Two duplicate shapes are linked side by side. The outer shapes have a Black or White Fill. The linkage has a Black or White Fill.

Answers

3) **d** - The number of enclosed shapes is equal to the number of sides of the outer shape. The enclosed shapes have the same rotation as the outer shape. The enclosed shapes have a Black or White Fill.
4) **d** - The Triangle is a rotation of the Test Figures.
5) **c** - The line ending is a Square with a Black Fill. The Square Line Ending is enclosed in the larger section of the Ellipse. The Circle has a Black or White Fill and is enclosed in the smaller section of the figure. When the Circle has a Black Fill, the Vertical Line is attached to the Horizontal Line.
6) **e** - The shape rotates 90° anticlockwise from top to bottom.
7) **d** - Two smaller shapes overlay a large shape. The three shapes are different. The total number of sides is 13.
8) **d** - There are six Quadrants. Two have a Black Fill, two have a Mottled Fill, one has a White Fill and one has a Lined Fill. There is one Quadrant with a Black Fill on each side.
9) **a** - The enclosed shape is a replica of the outer shape with a 90° clockwise rotation. The enclosure is in the half of the shape with a White Fill. The enclosure has a Black or Grey Fill and the other half has a Black or Grey Fill. There is one Grey and one Black Fill.
10) **b** - There are five Black Fills and three White Fills. There are three Square Line Endings and five Circle Line Endings.

Non-verbal Reasoning Test 3
Section A

Example - **d** - O - Arrow points upwards; W - Horizontal Lined Fill

1) **a** - M - One shape; J - Cross
2) **c** - S - Large figure; R - Arrow points downwards
3) **d** - F - Small figure; S - Grey Fill
4) **e** - K - Moon Shape is over the Wizard's Hat Shape; Q - Wizard's Hat Shape points upwards
5) **c** - B - Three Lines; F - Circle Line Ending with a Black Fill
6) **a** - E - Chevron Shape points left; U - Thick Outline
7) **b** - J - Three Quadrants with a White Fill; M - Grey Fill
8) **d** - D - Four sections; K - Small figure
9) **b** - B - Sector; P - Horizontal Lined Fill

Section B

Example - **a** - Solved horizontally: The figure has been rotated 90° clockwise. The Black Fill has become Grey.

1) **e** - The matrix is symmetrical.
2) **b** - Solved vertically: The shape has been rotated 45° anticlockwise. The White Fill has become Grey.
3) **a** - Solved vertically: The top shape has been flipped vertically. The outline of the bottom shape has become Dashed.
4) **a** - Solved horizontally: The figure has been rotated 90° clockwise and reduced in size. The Lined Fill has been rotated 90°. A new outer shape has been added.
5) **c** - Solved horizontally: The figure has been flipped horizontally. The fills have been swapped.
6) **d** - Solved vertically: The shapes have been moved two places clockwise. The fills have been moved one place clockwise.
7) **c** - Solved horizontally: There must be one figure with one shape, one figure with two shapes and one figure with three shapes. There must be one Black Fill, one White Fill and one Grey Fill.
8) **a** - Solved vertically or horizontally: There must be one Thin Outline, one Thick Outline and one Dashed Outline. The shapes must be the same orientation.

Section C

Example - **b** - The figure rotates 90° clockwise. One Arrow is subtracted.

1) **e** - The figure rotates 90° anticlockwise. The Dashed and Solid Outlines swap. One Circle is removed.
2) **c** - One side is added. The fill rotates 45° anticlockwise.

Answers

3) **d** - One Line is subtracted anticlockwise. The line type alternates between Solid and Dashed.
4) **b** - The order of fills of the Star is: Black, Grey, White, Black, Grey. The Quadrant rotates 90° anticlockwise. The order of fills of the Quadrant is: Grey, White, Black, Grey, White. The Crosses keep the same orientation.
5) **e** - The size order is: large, medium, small, large, medium. The order of fills is: Black, Grey, White, Black, Grey. The Speaker Shape rotates 90° clockwise.
6) **c** - One Line is added. The figure is rotated 90° clockwise. The fill of the Circle on the middle Line alternates between Black and White. The line endings alternate between Circle and Square.
7) **b** - The figure rotates 45° anticlockwise. The fills move one position clockwise.
8) **a** - The Arrow rotates 90° clockwise. The corners rotate 90° anticlockwise.
9) **c** - The figure flips horizontally then vertically alternately. The figure reduces then enlarges alternately. The order of fills is: Grey, Black, White, Grey, Black.
10) **b** - The Cross rotates 45°. One Hexagon is added in size order. The order of fills is: Black, Speckled, White, Black, Speckled.

Section D

Example - **d** - The figure is not Straight-edged.

1) **c** - The shapes are not different.
2) **e** - The enclosed shapes are not all the same size or all different sizes.
3) **e** - The top shapes are not different.
4) **c** - The fill is not Vertical or Horizontal Lined.
5) **e** - The shape is not Curved.
6) **d** - The shape does not have a line of symmetry.
7) **e** - The figure does not contain five Circles with a White Fill and three Circles with a Black Fill.
8) **d** - There is no section containing three Crosses.

Non-verbal Reasoning Test 4

Section A

Example - **d** - The figure rotates 90° clockwise. The fill becomes White.

1) **d** - The figure rotates 90° clockwise. The White Fill becomes Grey. The Black Fill becomes White.
2) **a** - The original shape becomes the top shape. A duplicate with a Thin Outline is added as the middle linkage. A duplicate with a Dashed Outline is added as a bottom linkage.
3) **c** - The shapes swap. The outer Line becomes Dashed.
4) **b** - The figure rotates 90° clockwise. The outer Line becomes Thin. The inner Line becomes Dashed.
5) **b** - The fills swap. The Lined Fill rotates 90°. The figure then rotates 180°. The new bottom shape rotates a further 90° clockwise.
6) **d** - The fills of the top two shapes swap. The bottom two shapes swap positions. The new bottom right shape flips vertically.
7) **c** - The figure rotates 45° anticlockwise. The Line with two endings with a White Fill becomes a Line with two endings with a Black Fill.
8) **e** - The figure rotates 90° clockwise. Another line of symmetry is added. The original Line becomes Thick. The outline becomes Dotted.
9) **e** - The figure flips vertically. A replica of the original shape with a Black Fill is added as an enclosure. The outline becomes Thick.

Section B

Example - **a** - Solved horizontally: The figure has been rotated 90° clockwise. The Black Fill has become Grey.

1) **d** - Solved horizontally: The figure has been reduced in size and has been rotated 90° anticlockwise.
2) **a** - Solved horizontally: The figure has been flipped horizontally. The outline has become Dashed.

Answers

3) **a** - Solved horizontally: The figure has been rotated 45°. The fills have been swapped.
4) **a** - Solved horizontally: The figure has been rotated 90° clockwise. One smaller Line with the same line ending has been added. The fill has become Black.
5) **e** - Solved horizontally and vertically: The figure has been rotated 90° clockwise. A Triangle has been enclosed in the House Shape alternately. The Dashed Outline and Solid Outline of the House Shape have been alternated. The fill of the Bow Tie Shape has been alternated between Grey and White.
6) **e** - Solved horizontally: There must be one Shield Shape pointing upwards, one Shield Shape pointing left and one Shield Shape pointing right. There must be alternating Black and White Fills. There must be one small, one medium and one large shape.
7) **c** - Solved vertically: The shape in row 1 has become the bottom shape of row 2 and has been rotated 180°. The shape in row 3 has become the top shape in row 2 and has been rotated 180°.
8) **b** - Solved horizontally: There must be one figure with one outer shape, one figure with two outer shapes and one figure with three outer shapes. There must be one figure with a Black Arrow enclosed, one figure with a Black Circle enclosed and one figure with no enclosure. There must be one Flower Shape, one Loaf Shape and one Hexagon lying on its side.

Section C

Example - **c** - A - Circle; Y - Grey Fill

1) **d** - Y - Pulley Shape; L - Concave Shield Shape
2) **a** - K - Horizontal figure; B - Small figure; G - Speckled Fill
3) **b** - X - Thin Outline; F - Enclosed Flower Shape; O - Outer Star Shape
4) **d** - A - Sector has a Grey Fill; E - Boat Shape has a Black Fill; Q - Boat Shape is large
5) **d** - T - Plus Shape; Z - Outer Shape is a Pentagon; G - Two enclosed shapes
6) **c** - L - One shape; F - Square Line Ending has a Black Fill; U - Figure points to the left
7) **b** - L - Quadrant has a Black Fill; X - Right angle has a Mottled Fill; A - Top-right Quadrant
8) **a** - S - Dashed Outline; C - Star on top; M - 5-pointed Star; Z - Ellipse

Section D

Example - **a** - The shape has four sides.

1) **d** - The shape is Curved with a Solid Outline and a line of symmetry.
2) **c** - The shape is part of a Circle with a White Fill.
3) **a** - There are two enclosed Horizontal Lines and an enclosed Star. The Shield Shape is convex.
4) **b** - The order of fills from the top is: Grey, White, Black. The shapes overlay vertically.
5) **e** - The figure has a Horizontal Lined Fill.
6) **e** - The enclosure is a 90° anticlockwise rotation of the outer shape. The shapes have a Black Fill and White Fill.
7) **d** - There is one Curved shape and one Straight-edged shape. The enclosure has a Black or Grey Fill.
8) **c** - The number of shapes is equal to the number of sides.
9) **b** - The outline is Dashed. There is more than one line of symmetry.
10) **b** - The Arrow is a rotation of the Test Figures. The Squares have a Grey or Black Fill. The Circle has a Grey or White Fill.

Non-verbal Reasoning Test 5
Section A

Example - **b** - The figure rotates 90° clockwise. One Arrow is subtracted.

1) **d** - The figure rotates 45° anticlockwise and flips horizontally, then rotates 45° anticlockwise and flips vertically, alternately.

Answers

2) **c** - The number of line endings is: 8, 6, 4, 2, 8. The Grey and White Fills alternate. The Pulley Shape remains in the same orientation.
3) **a** - The figure rotates 90° clockwise. The outlines are: Dashed, Solid, Dotted, Dashed, Solid. The order of the fills of the Circles is: White, Grey, Black, White, Grey.
4) **b** - The figure rotates 90° anticlockwise. The Black and White Fills alternate. One Bone Shape is added clockwise.
5) **a** - The order of shapes is: Circle, Square, Triangle, Circle, Square. The central enclosed outline alternates between Thick and Thin. One shape is added enclosing the figure.
6) **d** - The order of fills of the Circles is: White, Black, Grey, White, Black. One Line is removed and one Circle is added.
7) **b** - The number of Bars on the Line is: 6, 4, 2, 6, 4. The shape on the right becomes the shape on the left of the next figure.
8) **d** - The outer shape becomes the enclosed shape of the next figure, and rotates 90° clockwise. The inner fill becomes the outer fill of the next figure.
9) **e** - The Cross moves one corner clockwise. The Black and White Fills alternate. The number of Pencil Shapes increases by 1. The Pencil Shapes alternate between pointing upwards and pointing downwards.

Section B

Example - **d** - The figure rotates 90° clockwise. The fill becomes White.

1) **c** - The shape horizontally reflects and reduces in size. The Solid Outline becomes Dashed. A Square with a Black Fill is added as an enclosure.
2) **b** - The shape flips vertically. The fills swap.
3) **a** - The shapes move one place clockwise. The top left shape rotates 90° anticlockwise before moving. The fills move one place anticlockwise.
4) **e** - The number of shapes enclosed is equal to the number of shapes in the original figure. The number of sides of each of the enclosed shapes is equal to the number of shapes in the original figure. The original shape becomes the outer shape. The fills become Black.
5) **d** - The large shape rotates 90° clockwise and reduces in size. The two outer shapes are removed. The remaining shape takes the fill of the original top right shape.
6) **c** - The figure rotates 90° anticlockwise. A new shape is added around the figure with the fill of the enclosed shape.
7) **a** - The shape rotates 180° and a duplicate is added. The fill becomes Black.
8) **b** - The figure rotates 90° anticlockwise and squashes. A duplicate of the original shape with a Speckled Fill is added behind.

Section C

Example - **d** - The figure is not Straight-edged.

1) **e** - The Triangle is not the same rotation as the others.
2) **b** - The Cross with a Black Fill does not have a 45° rotation.
3) **b** - The smaller shapes do not have one less side than the larger shape.
4) **c** - The enclosed shape is not an anticlockwise rotation of the outer shape.
5) **d** - The Arrows do not point in the same direction.
6) **b** - There are not more Triangles or Squares than Circles.
7) **c** - The Thick Line is not a line of symmetry.
8) **a** - The two figures are not 180° rotations of each other.

Section D

Example - **d** - O - Arrow points upwards; W - Horizontal Lined Fill

1) **c** - T - White Fill; B - One enclosed shape
2) **a** - H - Moon Shape faces upwards; M - Moon Shape has a White Fill
3) **e** - A - Heart Shape; X - House Shape

Answers

4) **d** - F - Small shape is above the Rectangle; L - Square
5) **b** - V - Three shapes; H - Semi-circle
6) **d** - B - Outer shape has a Black Fill; H - Enclosed shape has a Grey Fill
7) **d** - E - Square Line Ending has a Black Fill; P - Solid Line
8) **a** - U - Quadrant; H - Two shapes
9) **c** - Q - Dashed Outline; N - White Fill
10) **b** - K - Mottled Fill; S - Small figure

Non-verbal Reasoning Test 6

Section A

Example - **a** - The shape has four sides.

1) **e** - The figure is Straight-edged. It has a Liquid Fill and a vertical line of symmetry.
2) **a** - There is an even number of Crosses enclosed. The number of enclosed Crosses is less than the number of sides of the outer shape.
3) **c** - The number of linkages is equal to the number of sides. Two of the shapes must only link to one other shape.
4) **a** - The figure has three Circle Line Endings with a Black Fill.
5) **d** - There are four enclosed shapes. One enclosure is a regular version of the outer shape and has a White Fill. Two of the enclosed shapes are the same and have a White Fill. One of the enclosed shapes has a Grey Fill.
6) **b** - The shape has six sides. The outline is either Thick Solid or Thin Dashed.
7) **b** - The enclosed shape has a Grey Fill. There is one Curved Shape and one Straight-edged Shape.
8) **d** - The linked shape on the right is a 90° anticlockwise rotation of the other shape.
9) **c** - The shape is the same orientation as the Test Figures. There is one Grey, one Black and one White Fill.

Section B

Example - **a** - Solved horizontally: The figure has been rotated 90° clockwise. The Black Fill has become Grey.

1) **e** - Solved vertically: The outline has become Dashed. A duplicate of the original with a 180° rotation has been added above as a linkage. A smaller replica of the original has been added as an overlay to the bottom.
2) **d** - Solved horizontally: The shape has been increased in size and has been rotated 90° anticlockwise.
3) **a** - Solved vertically: A duplicate of the figure with a 180° rotation has been added and these merge centrally. The fill of the top shape has become Black. The top and bottom shapes have been joined by a Thick Solid Line.
4) **c** - Solved horizontally: The top left shape has been flipped horizontally. The top right shape has become Grey. The bottom two shapes have been swapped. The new bottom left shape has been rotated 90° anticlockwise and the outline has become Thick. The new bottom right shape has been rotated 90° anticlockwise.
5) **b** - Solved vertically: Half of the top shape has been removed. The fills have been swapped. The bottom shape has been stretched and flipped horizontally. A Thick Solid Cross has been added behind the figure.
6) **a** - The matrix is symmetrical.
7) **c** - Solved vertically: The shape in row 1 has been rotated 90° anticlockwise and enclosed in the shape in row 2 to make the figure in row 3. The outer shape in row 2 has been rotated 90° anticlockwise. The fills of the shapes have been swapped.
8) **d** - Solved horizontally: There must be one small, one medium and one large shape. There must be two White Fills and one Lattice Fill. The Curved Arrow has been rotated 90° anticlockwise.

Section C

Example - **b** - The figure rotates 90° clockwise. One Arrow is subtracted.

1) **a** - The figure rotates 90° anticlockwise. The fill alternates between Lined and Grey. The Lined Fill rotates 90°.

Answers

2) **c** - The figure rotates 45° clockwise. The order of outlines is: Thin, Medium, Thick, Medium, Thin. The Star alternates between the bottom and top of the shape.
3) **d** - The shape alternates between a Cross and a Spike Shape. The Cross rotates 45°. The order of fills is: Black, Grey, White, Black, Grey.
4) **e** - The order of shapes is: Circle, Bone Shape, Star, Circle, Bone Shape. The fill alternates between Speckled and Lined. The order of size is: Large, Large, Small, Small, Large.
5) **b** - One Square is added and one Circle is added. The Squares alternate between left and right. The fill of the Circles alternates between Black and White.
6) **b** - The figure alternates between vertical and horizontal. The order of fills is: White, Black, Grey, White, Black. One Hexagon is subtracted.
7) **a** - The figure rotates 90° clockwise. The enclosed shape alternates between Square and Circle. The order of outlines is: Dotted, Solid, Dashed, Dotted, Solid.
8) **d** - The number of Heart Shapes is: 3, 2 1, 4, 3. The Heart Shapes are removed clockwise. The figure rotates 90° clockwise.
9) **a** - The figure rotates 90° clockwise. The Triangle alternates between top and bottom. The fill alternates between Left Slant Lined and Right Slant Lined.
10) **c** - The line endings alternate between Square and Circle. One more flips horizontally. The figure rotates 180°.

Section D

Example - **c** - A - Circle; Y - Grey Fill
1) **e** - F - Bulb Shape faces downwards; M - Enclosed shape is a Triangle
2) **c** - C - White Fill; Q - Four sections; X - Small figure
3) **a** - G - Figure points to the left; T - White Fill
4) **c** - W - Flower Shape is upright; G - Circle has a Grey Fill; B - Flower Shape has a Vertical Lined Fill
5) **e** - K - Pentagon points to the right; Q - Pentagon has a Dashed Outline; A - Outer shape is a Square
6) **a** - R - Grey Fill; N - Circle; F - Vertical figure
7) **b** - X - Large figure; C - Grey Fill; R - Helmet Shape faces downwards
8) **d** - Y - Grey Fill; C - House Shape points to the left; L - Dotted Outline; Q - Outer shape is a Diamond

Non-verbal Reasoning Test 7
Section A

Example - **d** - O - Arrow points upwards; W - Horizontal Lined Fill
1) **e** - Q - Blade Shapes face in opposite directions with the straight edges in the middle of the square; S - Two White Fills
2) **c** - M - Plus orientation; X - Grey Fill
3) **d** - W - Black Fill is at the top; L - Figure is in the middle of the square
4) **a** - G - Spike Shape points to the right; M - Three enclosed Lines
5) **a** - U - Flower Shape has a Lined Fill; D - Circle has a Black Fill
6) **e** - M - Arrow is positioned at the bottom right; A - Arrow points to the bottom left
7) **b** - X - Outer shape has a Thin Solid Outline; F - Enclosed shape has a Dashed Outline
8) **a** - P - Enclosed Line is a Wave; U - Outer shape is a Loaf Shape
9) **e** - F - Loaf Shape faces downwards; B - Enclosed shape has a White Fill

Section B

Example - **d** - The figure rotates 90° clockwise. The fill becomes White.
1) **d** - The outline becomes Thick Solid. A duplicate with a 90° anticlockwise rotation is added as a merger.
2) **e** - The Black Fill becomes White. The Line becomes enclosed vertically and extends to the full length of the shape. The shape is enclosed at the centre. The outer shape rotates 90°.

Answers

3) **c** - The Churn Shape becomes a Loaf Shape. The Square becomes a Triangle. The Solid Outline becomes Dashed.
4) **b** - The shapes move one position downwards. The fills move one position upwards. The original top shape flips horizontally. The original middle shape rotates 90° clockwise.
5) **e** - The figure rotates 90° clockwise. The enclosed Line transposes. The Square Line Ending becomes a Circle.
6) **d** - The figure horizontally reflects. A smaller replica of the Set Square Shape with a 180° rotation is added. The smaller Set Square Shape has the fill of the original shape. The Black Fill becomes Grey.
7) **b** - The shape increases in size. A duplicate with a 90° rotation and a Horizontal Lined Fill is added as an overlay.
8) **b** - The figure rotates 90° anticlockwise. The Dashed Line becomes Solid. The Black Fill becomes Grey. The new top shape flips vertically. The White Fill becomes Lined.

Section C

Example - **a** - Solved horizontally: The figure has been rotated 90° clockwise. The Black Fill has become Grey.

1) **d** - Solved horizontally: The bottom left shape has become the outer shape with a Thin Solid Outline. The top shape has been rotated 45° anticlockwise. The top and bottom shapes have been swapped and flipped as one. The top enclosed shape must have the line type of the original bottom left shape.
2) **e** - Solved horizontally: The fill has been moved one position inwards. The outline order from the centre Circle must be: Thick, Thin, Thick, Thin.
3) **e** - Solved horizontally: The figure has been reflected along the vertical mid-line of the matrix. The outlines of the outer and enclosed shapes have been swapped. The enclosed shape has been rotated 90° clockwise and has been reduced in size. The Circle has become an enclosure.
4) **c** - Solved vertically: The shapes have been swapped. The new bottom shape has been flipped vertically. The fills have been swapped. The Lined Fill has been rotated 90°.
5) **b** - Solved vertically: The outer shape has been vertically flipped along the horizontal mid-line of the matrix. The Grey Fill has become White. The Open Arrow Ending has become Closed. The Arrow has been rotated 180°.
6) **d** - Solved horizontally: There must be one Spike Shape, one Speaker Shape and one House Shape. There must be one White Fill, one Mottled Fill and one Black Fill. The shapes have been pointed in different directions.
7) **a** - Solved horizontally: There must be one White Fill, one Black Fill and one Grey Fill. There must be one figure with one shape, one figure with two shapes and one figure with three shapes. There must be one Star, one Heart Shape and one Flower Shape.
8) **b** - Solved horizontally: The figure has been rotated 90° anticlockwise. The White and Grey Fills have been alternated.

Section D

Example - **a** - The shape has four sides.

1) **d** - The outer shape flips vertically and the enclosed shape changes fill to form the bottom shape. The Grey Fill is in the top shape.
2) **e** - There is one shape with a Black Fill at the top left. There is one shape with a Dashed Outline at the bottom right. The Flower Shape has a 45° rotation. The enclosed shapes are a Cross, a Triangle, a Flower Shape and a 6-pointed Star.
3) **e** - The overlay is a 180° rotation of the larger shape and has a Grey or Black Fill. The overlay is on the left or right, and not on a point.

Answers

4) **d** - There are three enclosed shapes. One has a Black Fill, the others are either both Grey Fill or both White Fill . The enclosed shape has one less side than the outer shape. The outline of the outer shape is Close Dashed.
5) **c** - One quarter of the shape has a Grey or Black Fill.
6) **a** - The number of sides of the enclosed shapes totals nine.
7) **e** - The Square is in the middle of the figure. The outer two shapes reflect.
8) **d** - The shape has been split in half vertically. Half of the shape has a Horizontal Lined Fill.
9) **b** - The enclosed line is Dashed. There are the same number of shapes on either side of the line. The outline is Dotted or Thin Solid.
10) **a** - The shapes have a 180° rotation. The fill rotates 90°.

Non-verbal Reasoning Test 8
Section A

Example - **a** - The shape has four sides.

1) **a** - The enclosed shape is a 90° anticlockwise rotation of the outer shape. The enclosed shape has a Grey or Black Fill. One of the shapes is Black.
2) **a** - There are three Triangle Arrowheads. There are two other line endings and one Line without a line ending.
3) **c** - The number of sides of the outer shape and the number of sides of the enclosed shape with a White Fill are the same. The enclosed shape with a Black Fill must be a Circle or a Square.
4) **b** - There are three enclosed Lines. The middle enclosed Line is Solid Thick. The outer two Lines are Thin. The Lines are lines of symmetry.
5) **e** - The central enclosed line is Dotted. One duplicate shape is an overlay and one duplicate shape is a linkage. The central enclosed line is vertical or horizontal.
6) **d** - The Arrow points clockwise and has a Lined Fill.
7) **b** - One side is added going downwards. The middle shape has a Horizontal Lined Fill.
8) **d** - The outer shape has a Liquid Fill. There is an enclosed Circle with a White Fill. The outer shape is Straight-edged and has an even number of sides.
9) **a** - The shape has one line of symmetry and has a Black or White Fill.

Section B

Example - **b** - The figure rotates 90° clockwise. One Arrow is subtracted.

1) **c** - The number of shapes alternates between two and one. The order of fills is: Grey, Grey, Black, Black, White.
2) **d** - The Quadrant flips horizontally. The outline alternates between Thick and Thin. The order of fills is: Black, White, Grey, Black, White. The Set Square Shape rotates 90° clockwise.
3) **d** - The order of superimpositions is: linkage, overlay, overlay, linkage, overlay. The Hexagon rotates 90°. The position of the Triangle is: top left, top right, bottom, top left, top right.
4) **b** - The fill of the previous outer shape becomes the fill of the next enclosed shape. The enclosed shape vertically flips.
5) **a** - One Square is added clockwise. The order of fills of the Cross is: White, Grey, Black, White, Grey. The fill of the Squares alternates between Left Slant Lined and Right Slant Lined.
6) **a** - The number of Arrows is equal to the number of sides of the next figure. The line type of the Arrow is the same as the next figure. The Arrows all face upwards.
7) **a** - One Circle with a White Fill moves from the next corner clockwise to the middle. The order of fills in the middle alternates between Black and Grey.
8) **e** - In pairs: the shapes swap. The Dashed Outline becomes Solid. The new enclosed shape rotates 90° anticlockwise.

Answers

9) **d** - The Horizontal Line Endings and Vertical Line Endings swap alternately. One Line is added horizontally then vertically alternately.
10) **b** - The order of sizes is: large, medium, small, medium, large. The fill alternates between Grey and Black. The Arrow rotates 90° anticlockwise.

Section C

Example - **d** - The figure is not Straight-edged.
1) **d** - The line ending is not in the large shape.
2) **c** - The small shape is not on the outside.
3) **e** - The shape is not part of a Circle.
4) **c** - The Arrow does not point clockwise.
5) **e** - There is no line of symmetry.
6) **c** - The Circle is not positioned at the base of the shape.
7) **d** - There is not a 6-sided shape enclosed.
8) **a** - The central shape is not the same size as the others.

Section D

Example - **c** - A - Circle; Y - Grey Fill
1) **d** - T - Semi-circle is rotated 180°; M - Black Fill
2) **b** - Q - Large figure; J - Black Fill; G - Parallelogram is vertical
3) **a** - X - Vertical; M - Two Line Endings with a Black Fill; S - Circle Line Ending
4) **d** - B - Squared Fill; S - Arrow is angled; G - Arrow points left
5) **d** - Y - Cross has a 45° rotation; M - Thin Outline; P - Medium-sized figure
6) **b** - R - Arrow points to the bottom right; B - Grey Fill; L - Triangle Line Ending
7) **c** - B - Enclosed shape has Thin Outline; L - Outer shape is an Ellipse; Y - Outer shape has Dashed Outline; D - Enclosed shape is a 5-pointed Star
8) **a** - D - Loaf Shape has a Grey Fill; N - Wizard's Hat Shape has a Black Fill; C - Loaf Shape points downwards; G - Wizard's Hat Shape faces upwards

Notes

PROGRESS CHARTS

Test 1

Section A	(9)	____
Section B	(8)	____
Section C	(8)	____
Section D	(10)	____
Total Score	______	
Percentage	______%	

Test 2

Section A	(8)	____
Section B	(9)	____
Section C	(8)	____
Section D	(10)	____
Total Score	______	
Percentage	______%	

Test 3

Section A	(9)	____
Section B	(8)	____
Section C	(10)	____
Section D	(8)	____
Total Score	______	
Percentage	______%	

Test 4

Section A	(9)	____
Section B	(8)	____
Section C	(8)	____
Section D	(10)	____
Total Score	______	
Percentage	______%	

Test 5

Section A	(9)	____
Section B	(8)	____
Section C	(8)	____
Section D	(10)	____
Total Score	______	
Percentage	______%	

Test 6

Section A	(9)	____
Section B	(8)	____
Section C	(10)	____
Section D	(8)	____
Total Score	______	
Percentage	______%	

Test 7

Section A	(9)	____
Section B	(8)	____
Section C	(8)	____
Section D	(10)	____
Total Score	______	
Percentage	______%	

Test 8

Section A	(9)	____
Section B	(10)	____
Section C	(8)	____
Section D	(8)	____
Total Score	______	
Percentage	______%	

Overall Percentage [%] **For the average add up % and divide by 8**

CERTIFICATE OF

ACHIEVEMENT

This certifies

____

has successfully completed

11+ Non-verbal Reasoning
Year 5–7

TESTBOOK **3**

Overall percentage score achieved ______ %

Comment ______________________________

____

Signed ______________________________
(teacher/parent/guardian)

Date ______________________________